MW01416639

REFLECTING UPON FEAR & FATE

Sir Ruff

© Copyright (2024) by
(SirRuffpublishing) - All rights reserved.

It is not legal to reproduce, duplicate, or transmit any part of this document in either electronic means or printed format. Recording of this publication is strictly prohibited.

This book is dedicated to:

The seekers of meaning in chaos and the finders of light in darkness.

TABLE OF CONTENTS

Introduction 5

The Nature of the Self 8

Reflections 1 16

Time and the Present Moment 22

Reflections 2 28

Love and the Soul's Longing 34

Reflections 3 42

Suffering and Endurance 49

Reflections 4 56

The Nature of Virtue 62

Reflections 5 69

Mortality 74

Reflections 6 86

Purpose and Destiny 90

Reflections 7 97

The Harmony of All Things 102

Reflections 8 110

Freedom and Acceptance 116

Reflections 9 122

Wisdom and Inner Peace 128

Reflections 10 134

Gratitude and the Gift of Life 139
Reflections 11 143
Solitude and Connection 149
Reflections 12 156
The Eternal Return 162
A Letter to the Self 169
About the Author 175

Introduction

Writing this book, has been an intimate journey, a journey not just through the themes that envelop our existence, but through the depths of my own soul. I invite you to join me as I unveil the reflections, insights, and revelations that emerged during this process. It is a journey marked by introspection, self-discovery, and, at times, profound fear.

From the moment I embarked on this journey, I was aware that I would be exposing not only my thoughts but also the raw emotions that accompany such a deeply personal exploration. Fear, in its many forms, has been a constant companion throughout my life. It has loomed large in the shadows, dictating my decisions and coloring my perceptions. The fear of judgment, of failure, and even of success has often silenced my voice. Yet, in the act of writing, I found an unexpected ally in vulnerability. By confronting my fears and laying them bare on the page, I began to understand their role in shaping not only my life but the lives of so many others.

I often found myself questioning the very nature of fate itself. Are we mere puppets, dancing to the strings of destiny, or do we hold the power to shape our own paths? This question haunted me as I wrote, pushing me to delve deeper into my experiences and the experiences of those around me. As I explored the concept of fate, I began to understand that it does not exist in a vacuum; it is influenced by our choices, our actions, and yes, our fears. It is a dynamic interplay, a dance that we are all engaged in, whether we are aware of it or not.

This process of writing has not been without its challenges. I've grappled with the fear of exposing my innermost thoughts, the fear that my words might not be enough, that they might not resonate, or that they might invite criticism. Yet, in facing these fears, I found the courage to push through, to embrace the discomfort of vulnerability. It is in that discomfort that growth occurs, and I have emerged from this journey transformed.

By sharing my reflections on fear and fate, I hope to create a space for dialogue a space where we can explore our shared humanity. My hope is that this book will serve as a catalyst for your own introspection, prompting you to examine the fears that hold you back and the fateful moments that have shaped your life. We are all on this journey together, and in our stories, we may find the connections that bind us. So, I invite you to take this journey with me. Together, let us reflect upon the fear that seeks to confine us and the fate that invites us to embrace the unknown. In doing so, may we uncover the profound truths that lie beneath the surface of our experiences and emerge with a deeper understanding of ourselves and our place in the world.

The Nature of the Self

The self, as I have come to understand it, is both more elusive and more present than I once believed. It exists in the moments between thought, in the space between the past and the future. It is the quiet witness to the outgoing tide and flow of emotion, and yet, this self, which seems so central to my existence, is remarkably difficult to define. I have tried to capture it in words, but words fail me. It slips through the net of language.

When I sit alone, removed from the world's noise, I am confronted with this question: who am I? At first, I am tempted to answer with labels. my name, role, and history. But these are merely external markers, worn like clothing that can be changed. Beneath them, I feel the stirrings of something more, something less easily defined. There is a sense of presence, a conscious awareness that persists even when all else disappears. I suspect this is the core of what it means to be me. And yet, this self is not static. It shifts and changes like the tides, molded by experience and shaped by time. The person I was yesterday is not the person I am today, and tomorrow will bring further change. Is there a true self, an unchanging essence that lies beneath the surface of these shifting identities? Or is the self nothing more than a collection of moments, each one fleeting and impermanent?

There is a paradox here. On one hand, the self feels deeply personal, something intimately tied to my own experience of the world. On the other hand, it is shaped by forces beyond my control, such as culture, biology, and circumstance. I did not choose the body I inhabit or the time into which I was born. I did not choose the events that have shaped my life. And yet, I must live with the consequences of these things. In some ways, the self feels like an accident of fate, a temporary manifestation of something far more significant than I can comprehend.

At times, I feel the weight of this realization. The self is not as solid or as permanent as I once believed. It is fragile, vulnerable to the whims of life. And yet, in this fragility, there is also a certain beauty. The self, like all things, is transient. It rises and falls like the breath, like the cycles of nature. To cling to it, to try to hold it in place, is to resist the natural flow of existence. But to accept its impermanence is to find peace in the ever-changing dance of life.

In moments of stillness, I have glimpsed something beyond the self, a vastness, an openness that is not bound by the limitations of individuality. It is as though the boundaries between myself and the world dissolve, and I am left with the sense that I am part of something far greater than the small self I usually identify with. This feeling is both humbling and liberating. It reminds me that the self, as important as it may seem, is not the whole of who I am.

Perhaps the true nature of the self lies in this paradox: that we are both individual and universal, both finite and infinite. We are the wave and the ocean, the breath and the air. To know oneself is to understand this duality, to embrace both the unique and the collective aspects of existence. It is to recognize that the self is not something to be grasped, but something to be lived.

The more I reflect on the nature of the self, the more I realize how little I truly understand. It is a mystery, one that deepens the more I explore it. But perhaps that is the point. The self is not something to be solved or fully known. It is something to be experienced, to be lived through in all its complexity and contradiction.

    I sit with this mystery. I allow myself to be both the questioner and the question, both the seeker and the sought. In this space of reflection, I find a quiet acceptance. I may never fully understand the nature of the self, but I can live with the uncertainty. After all, the self is not a destination it is a journey, one that unfolds with each moment, with each breath.

    In the end, the self is not something to be found but something to be realized. It is the awareness that exists in the space between thought, the presence that endures through all change. To know the self is not to define it, but to be it to live with open awareness, to embrace the mystery of existence, and to find peace in the ever-changing flow of life.

    There was a time in my life when I became a stranger to myself, chasing the question of who I was with such desperation that I lost sight of the person I used to be. It began when I felt like every identity I once wore—son, friend, lover—began to fracture, each piece breaking away as I sought answers from places that held none. I remember looking in the mirror and not recognizing the person staring back. My days were filled with self-doubt, an insatiable urge to redefine my existence, and a persistent fear that I might never find what I was looking for.

In this search for myself, I clung to relationships that felt like lifelines, hoping others could help fill the void I could not explain. Yet, in trying to mirror those around me, I only felt emptier. I molded myself into versions of what I thought others wanted—a chameleon in a sea of expectations. I wore the smiles that people wanted to see, hid the parts of me that I thought were unworthy, and pushed forward, even when each step felt like sinking deeper into an unrelenting fog.

One of the hardest parts was the growing realization that I had neglected my own beliefs and passions. I started discarding pieces of myself in favor of fleeting validation. Hobbies that once brought me joy felt irrelevant, and pursuits that once defined me were now secondary to the goal of finding acceptance in the eyes of others. This dissonance between who I was and who I pretended to be became overwhelming, and there were days when all I felt was the heaviness of my own uncertainty.

It wasn't until I hit a breaking point that the weight of my own confusion became too much to bear. I felt the hollow ache of having no answers, only an endless stream of questions. The relationships I leaned on became strained because the person they knew wasn't me anymore, and I resented their well-meaning questions about what was wrong. I could never articulate it then, but the truth was, I wasn't just lost I was lost within myself, wandering in circles trying to become someone I didn't even recognize. There came a moment of painful clarity during a solitary drive one night. I pulled over on a quiet road, staring into the dark expanse, and realized that in trying to redefine myself, I had neglected the person I already was. I was always searching for a "new" me, assuming that my old self wasn't enough. It dawned on me that my struggle wasn't about changing who I was—it was about accepting that who I was already whole, flaws and all.

The road back to myself was not a sudden turnaround but a slow and deliberate walk-through familiar place within. I had to let go of the idea that I needed to find a perfect version of myself to be content. It was about acknowledging my imperfections, forgiving myself for losing sight of them, and reclaiming the things I once loved but had abandoned in my pursuit of reinvention.

Looking back, I learned that sometimes we seek ourselves in the wrong places. We look for answers in the expectations of others or the fleeting approval of the crowd. We wear masks, forgetting that authenticity doesn't mean perfection but rather embracing who we are without apology. It took losing myself completely to understand that self-discovery isn't about becoming someone else; it's about finding comfort in who you already are.

In your search for identity, never forget that you are already enough. Growth and change are inevitable, but they do not require losing yourself in the process. It's not the search that matters but the honesty in which you allow yourself to be seen, even in moments of doubt and vulnerability.

Sometimes, the person we're looking for is waiting in the places we've always known but have been too afraid to revisit.

Reflections 1

In the stillness of morning,
when the world is draped in a soft hush,
I stand before the mirror
a canvas of imperfection and light.
Here, I confront the myriad reflections,
each whispering a story,
a fragment of who I am,
yet none can contain the whole.

I am a mosaic of memories,
shards of laughter and tears,
an intricate puzzle,
each piece holding a secret,
a whisper of time.
The child who danced in puddles,
the lover who felt the weight of goodbyes,
the wanderer, searching for a home
in the wild expanse of the world.

In the depths of solitude,

I find echoes of my heart's
longing,
the yearning for connection
not just with others,
but with the essence of my
being,
the breath that flows through me,
the pulse of existence itself.
Who am I in the quiet moments,
when the masks slip away,
and I stand bare before my
thoughts?

I am the sum of my fears,
a fragile structure built on doubt,
yet also a beacon of resilience,
fueled by the flicker of hope.
I carry the weight of
expectations
society's demands,
family's dreams,
the relentless ticking of the
clock,
each tick a reminder of the fleeting
now.
And yet, within this chaotic dance,

I discover the beauty of
contradiction.
I am both the storm and the calm,
the chaos and the order.
In my laughter, I hold sorrow,
in my joy, a hint of melancholy.
I am a tapestry woven from
threads
of love
and threads of loss,
each thread is a testament to the
journey
that has brought me here.

There are days when I feel
fragmented,
lost in the noise of the world,
where the self seems to dissolve,
slipping through my fingers
like grains of sand.
In those moments, I seek refuge,
a quiet corner of my soul,
where I can hear the whisper of
my truth,
where the layers peel back,
and I can see the core of who I am.

It is in these spaces of reflection
that I confront my shadows,
the parts of myself I wish to
hide,
the doubts that linger like fog.
I sit with them,
not as enemies but as
companions,
for they have shaped me,
and in embracing them,
I begin to understand the
fullness
of my humanity.

As I navigate this labyrinth of
self,
I realize that I am not a
destination
but a journey a river,
constantly flowing,
ever-changing,
shaped by the landscape around
me,
yet deeply rooted in my essence.
I am the mountain and the valley,
the sunrise and the sunset,

an intricate interplay of light and
shadow.
In the dance of existence,
I find connection,
the threads that bind us all
the shared struggles, the triumphs,
the collective heartbeat of
humanity.
In recognizing our shared journey,
I dissolve the illusion of
separateness,
and in that moment,
I am not just myself,
but a reflection of us all.

As the day gives way to night,
I gather the pieces of my heart,
and I carry them forward,
embracing the complexities,
the joys and the sorrows.
For in the nature of the self,

I find not only the essence of
who I am
but the beauty of being
a beautiful chaos, a divine
uncertainty,
and ultimately,
the gift of existence itself.

Time and the Present Moment

Time is the framework through which we make sense of our existence, the measure by which we order our days and our lives. Yet, the more I reflect on time, the more I question whether it is something that exists outside of us or within us. We speak of time as though it is a force that moves us forward, propelling us from the past into the future. But in truth, time is always now. The past is nothing more than a memory, and the future nothing but a projection. Only the present moment is real.

I have spent much of my life either looking backward or forward, dwelling in what was or what might be. There is a certain comfort in revisiting the past, in replaying memories as though they might reveal some new insight or understanding. And in the future, how often have I found myself caught in its grip, planning, worrying, and anticipating what is to come? Yet, in these moments, I realize I am missing the present. It slips through my fingers unnoticed, lost in the endless cycle of thought about times that do not exist.

The present moment, when I am truly in it, is astonishing in its fullness. It is both infinite and fleeting. It contains everything, and yet it passes in the blink of an eye. When I bring my attention to the now, the world opens up in a way that is both startling and profound. Colors seem more vibrant, sounds more distinct, sensations more immediate. It is as though the present moment holds the entirety of life within it, and I have only just begun to notice.

living in the present is not as easy as it sounds. The mind is restless, constantly pulling me away from the now and into the realm of thought. It tells stories, replays conversations, plans for the future, and revisits the past. It is as though the mind is uncomfortable with the present, as though it fears the stillness that comes from being fully in the moment. And perhaps it does. To be fully present is to relinquish control, to let go of the narratives that define who I am and what my life is meant to be.

There is a kind of surrender in living in the present moment. It requires me to trust that life is unfolding exactly as it should, that there is nothing more I need to do than simply be here, now. And yet, this is incredibly difficult. The ego resists this surrender. It wants to define, to control, to predict. It wants to know what will happen next, to hold onto the past as though it might provide some sense of security. But the present moment offers none of these things. It offers only itself, raw and unfiltered.

In moments of true presence, I am stripped bare of all pretenses. There is no future to look forward to, no past to hold onto. There is only what is. And what is, I am beginning to realize, is enough. The present moment contains everything I need, if only I am willing to let go of the need to be elsewhere. This letting go, however, feels like a kind of death. It is the death of the ego, of the part of me that clings to the illusion of control, to the idea that I am the one steering the ship.

Time, I now see, is a construct of the mind. It is a way we attempt to grasp the ungraspable, to make sense of the flow of life. But in truth, there is no time outside of this moment. The past is a story we tell ourselves, a collection of memories that may or may not be accurate. The future is a projection, an imagined series of events that may never come to pass. Only the present is real, and even it is elusive, slipping away the moment we try to capture it.

There is a certain freedom in this realization. If the present is all there is, then there is no need to carry the weight of the past or the burden of the future. I can simply be here, now, and trust that life will unfold as it must. This does not mean that I ignore the lessons of the past or fail to plan for the future. But it means that I do not live in those places. I learn, I plan, and then I return to the now, where life is actually happening.

The present moment is always new, always fresh. It is untouched by the stories we tell ourselves, untainted by the regrets of the past or the fears of the future. It is pure experience, unmediated by thought. When I am in the present, I am alive in a way that is difficult to describe. There is a vibrancy, a clarity that cuts through the fog of habitual thinking. Everything becomes more real, more immediate. But this presence, this awareness of the now, is fragile. It is easily lost, swept away by the current of thought. I find myself constantly pulled back into the mind, into the stories it tells about who I am and what my life is. And yet, I know that the present is always here, waiting for me to return. It is patient, unchanging, always available, no matter how often I forget it.

There is a kind of paradox in the present moment. It is both fleeting and eternal. It is always changing, yet it never changes. The present moment is the same now as it was when I was a child, and it will be the same when I am old. It is the only constant in a world of impermanence. Everything else comes and goes, but the present remains.

To live fully in the present moment is to live fully in life. It is to engage with the world as it is, not as I wish it to be. It is to see things clearly, without the filter of past experiences or future expectations. It is to be alive to the richness of each moment, to the beauty and the pain, the joy and the sorrow. All of it is contained in the now. And so, I strive to return, again and again, to the present. It is not a place I can stay permanently, for the mind will always pull me away. But I can come back, each time with a little more awareness, a little more understanding of the gift that the present moment offers. In the end, the present is all I have. It is all any of us have. And perhaps that is enough.

Reflections 2

Time, that elusive thread,
slips through my fingers,
a quiet river flowing unseen,
carving valleys in my soul
as I stand still, wondering
how to grasp its current,
how to hold what cannot be held.

Each second, a grain of sand,
falling, unnoticed,
until I look back at the hourglass of
my life,
the moments I thought infinite,
now nothing more than echoes.
I chase them, try to retrace my steps,
but they vanish into the wind
like whispers I can no longer hear.

We live between past and future,
always looking behind,
always straining ahead
forgetting, in our haste,
the delicate pulse of the present.

It's here, now, in the quiet
breath,
in the stillness between
heartbeats,
where life waits to be felt
in its fullness.

But the present is fleeting,
a blink,
a pause,
before the next rush of time
carries us forward.
It's like standing on the shore,
watching waves crash and
recede,
each one a moment that was, and
will never be again.
We cling to the past,
build monuments of memory,
forgetting that time,
like the sea,
never gives back what it takes.
And yet, it's in that letting go
that we find the beauty
the impermanence,
the fleeting joy of a sunrise

that will never rise the same way
twice.

The present moment is an
offering,
a gift wrapped in silence and
awareness,
but so often, we fail to open it.
We wait for something more,
something better,
forgetting that life is happening
in the spaces we overlook.
In the smell of rain,
the warmth of sunlight on skin,
the sound of laughter carried on
the wind.

Time does not wait for us to be
ready,
it moves, indifferent to our plans,
our fears, our desires.
It asks only that we pay
attention,
that we honor the now
before it slips into the past,
forever unreachable, no longer ours.

I think of all the moments I've missed,
the times I was too busy looking ahead,
too consumed by what could be,
to see what was.
And now I wonder:
how many sunsets passed unnoticed?
How many smiles went unseen?
How many moments of grace were lost
because I wasn't present enough to see them?

The present moment,
that fragile thread between what was
and what will be,
is where we find the truth of who we are.
It's in the stillness,
in the breath,
that we meet ourselves,
not as we were

or as we hope to be,
but as we are,
right here,
right now.

And in that meeting,
there is peace.
Not the peace of perfection,
but the peace of being,
of knowing that this moment
is all there ever truly is.
Time is a river,
and we are both the water
and the stone it shapes
molded by the moments we
choose to live
and the ones we let slip away.

In the present,
we are eternal,
if only for an instant.
A breath held in time,
a pause between thoughts.
Here,
we are everything,
and nothing at all.

Just the pulse of life
carried on the wings of time,
existing for a moment,
and then
gone.

So, I sit in the present,
feeling the weight of its
lightness,
its fragility,
and I wonder
what is time,
if not the mirror of our lives,
reflecting the fleeting beauty
of each moment we inhabit and
each one we let go.

Love and the Soul's Longing

I have come to realize that love is more than a feeling it is a force, an energy that flows through life, connecting everything it touches. It is elusive, often misunderstood, yet so fundamental to the human experience that to speak of life without love is to speak of a hollow existence. Love, at its deepest level, is the soul's longing to merge with something greater than itself. It is the desire to dissolve into the infinite, to lose oneself in the embrace of the whole, and in that dissolution, to be found.

This longing is not easily satisfied. We search for it in others, seeking in another's eyes the reflection of our own incompleteness. We hope that in the merging of two hearts, we might finally feel whole, that the ache of separation might be soothed. But this quest for love is often filled with both joy and suffering. It is like a desert traveler, desperate for water, chasing mirages across the endless sands. Every connection offers the promise of fulfillment, and yet, like the mirage, it disappears as soon as we try to hold onto it.

The soul's longing for love is like a bird searching for the wind. It flies tirelessly, seeking that invisible current that will lift it higher, that will carry it effortlessly toward the horizon. In moments, it feels the wind beneath its wings, and it knows it is part of something vast and boundless. But just as quickly, the wind shifts, and the bird is left flapping, struggling to stay aloft. This is the nature of love it is both the wind that lifts us and the absence that leaves us yearning.

In love, we experience the profound joy of connection, of being seen and known by another. But there is always an underlying tension, a sense that this connection, no matter how deep, can never fully satisfy the soul's infinite longing. No matter how close we come to another, there remains a space between us, a gap that cannot be bridged. And in that gap lies the bittersweet nature of love the joy of closeness, tempered by the ache of separation.

Perhaps this is because the soul's true longing is not for another person, but for something beyond the human experience of love. It is the desire to return to the source from which it came, to reunite with the infinite love that permeates the universe. Every act of love we experience in this world is but a reflection of that greater love, a dim echo of the soul's true home. And yet, we cling to the reflections, mistaking them for the source.

In moments of deep connection with another, it is as though the soul recognizes itself. There is a sense of coming home, of being whole for a brief instant. But this feeling is fleeting, and it is in its fleeting nature that we come to understand the paradox of love. To truly love, we must accept that it cannot be possessed or held. Love, like water, flows where it will. To try and hold it is to watch it slip through our fingers. And yet, when we allow it to flow freely, we find that it fills us in ways we could never have anticipated.

The soul's longing for love is like a river seeking the ocean. It flows endlessly, carving its path through the landscape of life, always moving toward something greater, something vast and unknown. Along the way, it encounters obstacles, but it continues its journey, for it knows that its destination lies beyond the horizon. The river may twist and turn, but it is always drawn toward the ocean, toward the infinite embrace that awaits it.

And yet, the river does not reach the ocean by force. It flows patiently, knowing that every twist, every obstacle, is part of the journey. Love, too, cannot be forced. It cannot be demanded or controlled. It must be allowed to flow in its own time, in its own way. To love deeply is to trust in this process, to surrender to the flow, knowing that the soul's longing will eventually lead it home.

In moments of love, we catch glimpses of the ocean, of that infinite source that calls to us. We feel it in the embrace of a lover, in the gaze of a child, in the quiet companionship of a friend. But these moments are fleeting, like sunlight breaking through the clouds for just a moment before the sky closes again. And yet, these glimpses are enough to sustain us, to remind us of what we are truly seeking.

My journey began with a lingering sense of something missing, as though my soul was trying to whisper to me, but I couldn't quite grasp the words. It wasn't a loud call but a persistent ache that lingered in the quiet moments between life's busyness. On the surface, everything seemed fine—

accomplishments, relationships, the routine of responsibilities—but beneath it all was a deep, restless yearning that wouldn't leave me alone. I tried to ignore it at first, pushing forward with what seemed like a perfectly mapped-out life. But over time, the feeling only grew stronger, demanding that I pay attention to what I was missing within myself.

It wasn't until life began to unravel in unexpected ways that I started to confront the truth. Certain relationships that had been foundational for me began to change, revealing cracks that were no longer possible to ignore. There were losses that left me feeling more alone than I had ever been, and moments of disillusionment with the very roles and titles I once took pride in. Each of these shifts seemed to peel away a layer of my identity, leaving me feeling exposed and unsure of where to go from there. The longing for something deeper became impossible to deny, and the question of what it all meant became more urgent with each passing day.

I remember one night in particular when the weight of it all felt unbearable. I sat in the stillness of my room, overwhelmed by a sense of emptiness that I couldn't explain away. I tried to pray, tried to find solace in the familiar rituals that had once been a source of comfort. But instead of relief, I was met with silence—a silence that felt vast and unnerving. I couldn't run from it anymore. I had to confront the reality that somewhere along the way, I had lost touch with my own soul, and I wasn't sure how to find my way back.

The journey to reconnect with my soul was not a straightforward path. It wasn't marked by a sudden epiphany or a clear turning point but rather a series of small, sometimes painful steps toward reclaiming what I had neglected. I began to strip away the layers of who I thought I was supposed to be—the roles, the masks, the expectations of others—and slowly started to listen to the quiet voice within. There were moments when I felt like I was making progress, followed by days when I seemed to slip back into old patterns of doubt and fear. But each time I stumbled, I tried to remind myself that this was all part of the process.

There were long stretches where the only thing keeping me going was sheer perseverance, the stubborn refusal to give up even when everything felt hopeless. I had to dig deep and confront the parts of myself I had tried to bury—the wounds, the regrets, the unanswered questions about who I was and who I wanted to be. It was painful to face these things head-on, but I knew that avoiding them would only keep me stuck in the same cycle of emptiness. Slowly, I learned to sit with my pain without trying to rush past it, to accept that healing doesn't happen on a convenient timeline.

Over time, I began to find small glimpses of clarity amidst the uncertainty. Moments of stillness where I could feel a sense of connection to something greater than myself, a flicker of recognition that maybe, just maybe, my soul was still there waiting for me to come home. I started to find meaning in the simplest things—a quiet walk, a heartfelt conversation, a moment of genuine honesty with myself. These moments became like breadcrumbs on a long and winding path, guiding me toward a deeper understanding of who I was beneath all the noise and expectations.

The longing that once felt like a burden began to feel more like a compass, pointing me toward the places where I needed to be vulnerable and authentic. I came to see that this journey wasn't about arriving at some perfect destination but about learning to embrace my imperfections and uncertainties as part of the journey itself. It was about finding the courage to let go of the things that no longer served me, even when it meant facing the unknown with nothing but faith to hold on to.

Looking back, I realize that the perseverance it took to find my soul wasn't just about pushing through difficult times; it was about learning to trust that even when I felt lost, there was still a part of me that knew the way. It was about having the courage to listen to the longing within and the willingness to keep moving forward, even when the road seemed impossibly long. I've come to understand that this longing was never something to be feared or avoided but rather a reminder that my soul was always reaching for something deeper, something truer. And in that journey, I've found not just answers, but a sense of belonging within my own life.

Reflections 3

There is a quiet yearning
that hums beneath the surface,
a soft ache,
a whisper that rises in the
stillness of night
and lingers in the spaces
between words,
between breaths,
a pull toward something
just out of reach.

The soul longs,
not for the touch of a hand
or the sound of a voice,
but for something deeper,
more elusive
a place where it can rest,
where it can find its reflection
in the vast expanse
of what it means to be alive.

It is a thirst,
but not for water.
it is hunger,
but not for food.
It is the yearning for connection,
to belong to something greater
than ourselves,
to find the thread that ties us
to the stars,
to the earth,
to the heartbeat of the universe
itself.

The soul wanders,
searching through the moments
of our days,
looking for glimpses of eternity
in the ordinary.
It finds them in the curve of a
leaf,
the shimmer of light on water,
the echo of laughter
that feels like it was always
meant to be heard.
We try to fill this longing
with the noise of the world

with accomplishments,
possessions,
people.
But the soul's hunger
is not sated by what can be held,
what can be touched.
It craves what is beyond touch,
beyond time,
what exists in the quiet spaces
we so often forget to visit.

This longing pulls us forward,
drives us toward the unknown,
toward the questions that have
no answers.
Who am I?
Where do I belong?
What is this ache that rises in my
chest
when I look at the sky,
the stars burning like promises
I have yet to understand.

The soul remembers
what we have forgotten.
It remembers the music of the
spheres,
the dance of light and shadow
that exists beyond our daily
lives,
in a realm we can only glimpse
when the world falls silent
and we listen.

It is in these moments of quiet
that the soul speaks.
Not in words,
but in feelings
in the soft stirring of something
ancient,
something eternal,
that tells us we are more
than just the roles we play,
more than the bodies we inhabit,
more than the fleeting moments
that pass like leaves in the wind.
The soul longs for home,
but not a home we can find
on any map.

It longs for the place
where it was born,
the place it will return to,
a place of wholeness,
where every question dissolves
into knowing,
where every tear
is answered with a smile.

And yet,
this longing is not meant
to be fulfilled here.
It is the fire that keeps us
moving,
the compass that points us
toward truth,
toward love,
toward the essence
of what it means to be human.

We carry this longing
in our hearts,
a quiet reminder
that we are more than the sum
of our days.
It is the echo of the divine,

calling us back
to the source,
to the light
that shines in the spaces
between our fears,
our doubts,
our fleeting desires.

The soul longs,
and in that longing,
it lives.
It searches,
it hopes,
it believes
in something more,
something just beyond
the edge of what we can see,
what we can touch.
And in that belief,
we find our way.

For the soul's longing
is not a weakness,
but a gift.
It is the bridge
between what is

and what could be,
the thread that ties us
to the infinite,
the unseen,
the eternal.

And so, we wander,
guided by this quiet ache,
knowing that in the longing,
we are alive.
In the searching,
we find ourselves.
In the yearning,
we become
what we were always meant to be
not just human,
but part of the divine,
a reflection of the stars,
of the light
that burns within us all.

Suffering and Endurance

Suffering is interlaced into the very fabric of existence. It is an inevitable part of life, a shadow that follows us no matter how carefully we plan or how tightly we hold on to moments of happiness. There is a certain universal truth in suffering: it is the common thread that binds all human experience. We all endure it in some form, though it manifests differently for each of us. Some face physical pain, while others battle with the invisible scars of emotional wounds. And though we often think of suffering in terms of loss or injury, I have come to see that one of the deepest forms of suffering is the kind that arises from grief, especially the grief of those who are still alive.

To grieve someone who is not dead is one of the most painful and confusing experiences. There is no closure, no finality to mark the end of the relationship. Whether it is the loss of a friendship, a romantic relationship, or even the fading connection with a family member, the person is still there, living and breathing in the world, yet they are lost to you. This form of grief is a wound that doesn't heal in the usual way because the person you mourn continues to exist, just beyond your reach. It is a constant reminder of what once was, of what could have been, and of what is now forever altered.

I remember a time in my life when I mourned someone who wasn't dead. They had simply chosen a different path, a life that no longer included me. The initial shock of the separation felt like a part of my soul had been ripped away. But unlike the grief we feel when someone passes, there was no funeral, no final goodbye. Instead, I found myself haunted by their presence, seeing traces of them in my daily life, in the spaces they once occupied. It was a slow, aching kind of suffering one that didn't have a clear end, because as long as they existed, so did the hope, the question, the "what if?"

This type of grief is particularly cruel because it requires endurance without resolution. There is no one to say, "It's over now, you can move on." Instead, the grief lingers like a fog that never fully lifts. You are forced to learn how to coexist with the pain, to find a way to continue living while carrying the burden of absence. This, I believe, is one of the most profound lessons sufferings has to teach us: that life goes on, even when our hearts are broken, even when the world as we knew it has shifted irrevocably.

Endurance, in this sense, becomes not just a response to suffering, but a way of life. It is the quiet strength that allows us to keep moving forward, even when everything inside of us wants to stop. We learn to endure not because we are immune to pain, but because we have no other choice. Life demands that we keep going, and so we do. Over time, endurance becomes a kind of muscle that we build, a resilience that allows us to carry the weight of our suffering without collapsing under it.

In some ways, enduring suffering is like walking through a dense forest with no clear path. The trees are thick, the light barely filters through, and you feel as though you might be lost forever. But with each step, you learn to navigate the darkness. You may stumble, you may fall, but eventually, you begin to trust in your ability to keep going, even when you cannot see where the path will lead. This is the essence of endurance: it is not about having all the answers or knowing when the pain will end, but about trusting that you have the strength to survive, even in the unknown.

I have often found that the most painful suffering comes not from what happens to us, but from what we imagine could have been. The grief of those who are still alive is steeped in these unfulfilled possibilities the alternate versions of reality that we play over and over in our minds. We think about the conversations that were never had, the moments that were lost, the futures that will never come to pass. This kind of suffering is relentless because it is not anchored in the present, but in a thousand imagined scenarios that never came to be. And yet, even in this suffering, there is growth. There is something about enduring pain that changes us. It forces us to let go of the illusion of control, to accept the impermanence of life. We realize that no matter how tightly we hold on, some things are meant to slip through our fingers. And in this realization, there is a quiet kind of liberation. It doesn't take away the pain, but it allows us to live with it, to make peace with the fact that suffering is an inescapable part of the human experience.

Endurance also teaches us the power of perspective. In the midst of suffering, it is easy to feel as though the pain will never end, that we are trapped in a state of perpetual grief. But with time, we begin to see that suffering, like everything else, is temporary. It comes in waves—some days are harder than others, and some moments feel unbearable—but it does not last forever. There will be moments of light, even in the darkest of times. And it is these moments, however fleeting, that remind us that we are capable of enduring more than we ever imagined.

There is also a strange beauty in suffering, though it is hard to see in the moment. It strips away the superficial layers of life, forcing us to confront what truly matters. When we suffer, we are reminded of our vulnerability, of our humanity. We are reminded that life is fragile, that everything we love can be taken from us in an instant. And in this realization, there is a kind of clarity. Suffering sharpens our focus, helping us to see what is truly important and to let go of what no longer serves us.

I think about the people who have endured great suffering, those who have lost loved ones, homes, even their sense of self. And yet, they find a way to keep going. They wake up each day and put one foot in front of the other, even when it feels impossible. This is the quiet courage of endurance. It is not flashy or dramatic; it is the simple, steadfast act of continuing, of showing up for life, even when it feels like too much.

In the end, I believe that endurance is about faith, faith in the process, faith in ourselves, and faith that life, in all its complexity, will offer us moments of grace even in the midst of our suffering. We may not always understand why we suffer, and we may never get the closure we seek. But endurance is about trusting that we have the capacity to carry our pain, that we can survive the grief of those who are gone, whether through death or distance. And so, we endure. We carry our grief, we live with our suffering, and we continue to move forward. Not because the pain has gone away, but because we have learned to coexist with it. And in this coexistence, we find a new kind of strength, a new kind of resilience. This, perhaps, is the true gift of suffering: it breaks us open, but in that breaking, it allows us to grow in ways we never imagined.

Reflections 4

Suffering arrives uninvited,
a shadow at the door,
creeping into our lives
with quiet persistence,
wrapping itself around the heart,
tightening with every breath.

It is a weight we carry,
not always seen,
but felt deep in the bones,
in the spaces where joy once lived.
It lingers in the silence,
in the moments between smiles,
a reminder of what we've lost,
what we've endured.

We resist it,
try to outrun its grasp,
bury it beneath distractions,
but it finds us still,
in the dead of night,
in the pause between thoughts,

when we are too tired to keep
pretending
we are whole.
Suffering carves us out,
leaves us hollow,
exposed to the winds of life
that never seem to stop blowing.
But in that hollowing,
there is space
space for something new,
something we cannot see
in the midst of the storm.
Endurance is the quiet force,
the steady breath that keeps us
moving
when all we want is to stop,
to sit down and let the world
pass us by.
It is the whispered promise
that this pain, too, will fade,
that time, in its slow and gentle
way,
will smooth the rough edges
of our grief.
Endurance does not fight
the way suffering does.

It bends,
it yields,
it accepts the weight
and carries it anyway.
It teaches us that strength
is not in the absence of struggle
but in the choice to keep walking
even when the road is steep
and the night is long.

We endure not because we are
unbreakable,
but because we break
and rise again,
each time a little wiser,
a little softer in our
understanding
of what it means to be human.

Suffering strips away our
illusions,
reveals the raw truth of our
fragility,
and yet, it also shows us
the depth of our resilience.
In the darkest moments,

we discover the quiet flame
that refuses to be extinguished,
the part of us that persists even when
all else is lost.
Endurance is the act of holding on,
of believing,
even when belief feels like a
distant memory,
that there is light on the other side of
the darkness,
that this too,
like everything,
will pass.
And when the storm clears,
we find ourselves changed
not whole,
not unscarred,
but alive,
still breathing,
still here.

Suffering leaves its marks,
but endurance writes a different
story.
It speaks of courage,
of the quiet strength
found in simply surviving,
in choosing,
again and again,
to face the day
with whatever fragments of hope
we can gather.

We grieve not only for those
we've lost
but for the parts of ourselves
that have faded away
the innocence,
the certainty,
the belief in an easy path.
But even in that grief,
there is growth,
a deeper understanding
of what it means to love,
to lose, to live.
In the end,
suffering and endurance walk

hand in hand,
one giving shape to the other.
Through suffering,
we learn the depths of our
endurance,
and through endurance,
we transform our suffering
into something more
a testament to the quiet power
of the human spirit.
And so, we endure,
not because we must,
but because it is in our nature to
rise,
to seek the light,
even in the midst of the darkest
nights.
For in every breath we take,
there is the promise of another,
and in that promise,
we find the strength to carry on.

The Nature of Virtue

Virtue is a concept we often speak of yet struggle to define. It seems like something we instinctively know is good, something to aspire to, but the more we contemplate it, the more we realize its complexity. Virtue, at its core, is about moral excellence, which is striving toward what is noble, what is just, and what is good. Yet, these terms themselves are open to interpretation. In many ways, the pursuit of virtue is less about arriving at a destination and more about the journey itself a continual effort to live in alignment with principles that reflect our highest version of ourselves.

What makes virtue so challenging is that it often requires us to go against our natural inclinations. We are, by nature, creatures of desire. We seek comfort, pleasure, and ease, and we are often driven by our immediate wants and needs. Virtue, however, asks us to rise above these instincts, to act not according to what is easiest or most pleasurable, but according to what is right. In this way, virtue is not about suppressing our humanity, but about elevating it, about choosing the harder, but more honorable, path.

One of the fundamental virtues is courage. Courage is often misunderstood as the absence of fear, but in reality, it is the ability to act in spite of fear. It is the willingness to step forward when every part of you wants to retreat. Courage is required in all aspects of life, from facing physical danger to confronting uncomfortable truths about ourselves. It is perhaps one of the most foundational virtues because, without courage, none of the other virtues are possible. To live virtuously, we must first have the courage to confront the difficult, to face the unknown, and to risk failure.

Another central virtue is wisdom, which is more than just knowledge. It is the ability to apply knowledge in a way that is thoughtful and discerning. Wisdom allows us to see beyond the immediate and the surface, to grasp the deeper meaning of things. It is what enables us to make good decisions, to navigate the complexities of life with grace and understanding. But wisdom, like all virtues, is something that must be cultivated. It comes from experience, from reflection, and from a willingness to learn from both success and failure.

Justice is another virtue that holds a special place in the moral landscape. It is the virtue that seeks fairness, that strives to give each person their due. Justice requires us to look beyond our own interests and consider the needs and rights of others. It is not simply about following laws, but about understanding the spirit of those laws, and ensuring that we act with fairness and equity in all situations. Justice, in its truest form, is not blind, but deeply aware of the nuances of human experience, and it seeks to create balance in a world often filled with imbalance.

Then there is the virtue of temperance or self-control. In a world that constantly pushes us toward excess whether in consumption, indulgence, or ambition temperance asks us to find balance. It is the virtue that teaches us to master our desires, rather than being mastered by them. Temperance is not about denial or deprivation, but about moderation. It is the ability to enjoy life's pleasures without becoming enslaved by them. In this way, temperance is about freedom the freedom that comes from not being controlled by our appetites or impulses.

Compassion is another key virtue, one that is deeply tied to our sense of humanity. It is the ability to feel the suffering of others and to act with kindness and empathy. Compassion allows us to extend ourselves beyond the boundaries of our own lives, to care for others even when it is inconvenient or difficult. In a world where it is easy to become numb to the suffering around us, compassion reminds us that we are all connected, that our well-being is tied to the well-being of others. To live virtuously, we must cultivate a heart that is open to the needs and pain of others.

Humility is often considered one of the quieter virtues, but it is no less important. Humility allows us to see ourselves clearly, without the distortions of pride or ego. It reminds us that we are fallible, that we do not have all the answers, and that there is always room for growth. Humility is not about self-deprecation or thinking less of ourselves; rather, it is about recognizing our limitations and being open to learning from others. It is the virtue that allows us to listen, to admit when we are wrong, and to seek truth over validation.

Gratitude is a virtue that is often overlooked, yet it plays a vital role in living a good life. Gratitude is the ability to appreciate the gifts of the present moment, to recognize the abundance that surrounds us, even in times of difficulty. It shifts our focus from what we lack to what we have, and in doing so, it opens our hearts to joy. Gratitude, like all virtues, requires practice. It asks us to slow down, to reflect, and to consciously choose appreciation over dissatisfaction. In this way, gratitude is not just an emotion, but a way of being.

The pursuit of virtue is not without struggle. In fact, it is often through struggle that virtue is born. It is easy to be virtuous when life is simple, when there are no real challenges to our character. But it is in moments of hardship, when we are tested, that our true virtues—or lack thereof are revealed. Virtue asks us to act with integrity, even when no one is watching, even when it would be easier to take a different path. This is the essence of moral courage, and it is what separates virtue from mere convenience. Virtue also requires balance. To be virtuous is not to be rigid or dogmatic, but to navigate the complexities of life with a sense of moral flexibility. For example, there are times when justice must be tempered with mercy, when courage must be balanced with prudence. Virtue is not about adhering to a strict code, but about understanding the spirit of that code and applying it with wisdom and compassion. It is this balance that allows us to live virtuously in a world that is anything but simple.

One of the most profound aspects of virtue is that it is inherently relational. Virtue is not something we cultivate in isolation; it is something that is expressed in how we relate to others. Our courage, our compassion, our justice they all find their meaning in the context of community. Virtue, then, is not just about personal moral excellence, but about contributing to the greater good. It is about creating a world where all people can flourish, where justice, kindness, and wisdom are not just ideals, but lived realities.

Perhaps the greatest challenge of virtue is that it requires us to constantly strive for something beyond ourselves. It is not a goal we ever fully achieve, but rather a journey we are always on. There will be moments when we fall short, when we act out of fear or selfishness, when we fail to live up to our ideals. But the pursuit of virtue is not about perfection it is about progress. It is about committing to the path, even when we stumble, and continually seeking to align our actions with our highest values.

Reflections 5

Virtue stands quietly,
in the corners of our lives,
not loud,
not demanding,
but waiting
a soft flame that flickers
in the choices we make
when no one else is watching.

It is not the armor we wear,
not the sword we wield,
but the stillness within,
the quiet knowing
of what is right,
of what is good,
even when the world around us
whispers otherwise.

Virtue is the compass
that guides us through the fog,
the hand that reaches out
when no reward is offered,
when no one applauds.

It is the strength
in moments of weakness,
the truth spoken
in the silence of fear.

We search for it,
sometimes without knowing,
in the simple acts
a kind word,
a gentle hand,
the choice to listen
when it would be easier to turn
away.
Virtue,
in its quiet way,
asks only that we be present,
aware of the ripples
our actions send into the world.
It is not perfection,
not something to be worn as a
crown,
but a path we walk,
each step uncertain,
each moment a decision
to lean into the light
or to fall into the shadows.

Virtue is the courage to stand
when the ground shakes beneath
our feet,
to hold the line
when the wind blows strong,
to believe in the goodness
that resides,
sometimes hidden,
within each of us.

It is the quiet refusal to give in
to anger,
to pride,
to the easy path
that tempts with promises
of fleeting gain.
Virtue is not the absence of
fault,
but the willingness to rise,
to keep rising,
even after we fall.

It whispers in our hearts,
in the quiet moments before
sleep,

in the stillness of morning,
asking not for grand gestures
but for the steady hand
that chooses the right way
over the easy way,
again, and again.

Virtue is the friend
who speaks truth,
even when it stings.
It is the stranger
who gives without expecting,
the parent who loves without
condition,
the leader who serves
with no need for a throne.

It is the foundation
upon which we build
the best of what we are,
not in the eyes of others
but in the eyes of ourselves,
in the quiet chambers of our soul
where we face our own
reflection.

Virtue is the enduring light,
the small flame we carry with us,
through the trials,
through the dark nights,
through the moments when we wonder
if it even matters.

But it does.
It matters,
in the way a single stone
can change the flow of a river,
in the way a small kindness
can soften a heart,
in the way we choose,
moment by moment,
to be a little better,
a little truer,
to the voice within.

For in virtue,
we find not only the world we wish to see,
but the person
we are meant to be.

Mortality

Mortality is the great equalizer, the one truth that unites us all. From the moment we are born, we are moving inevitably toward our end. It is a fact that we often try to ignore or push aside, distracted by the busy demands of daily life. Yet, in quiet moments, when the distractions fade away, the awareness of our finite nature creeps back in. We are reminded that our time on this earth is limited, and that knowledge can either weigh heavily on us or inspire us to live with more intention. The awareness of mortality is both a burden and a gift.

What does it mean to live with the knowledge of death? How do we reconcile the inevitable end with the desire to live fully? These are questions that have plagued humanity since the dawn of consciousness. Some choose to deny mortality, to live as though death does not exist, while others fixate on it, allowing the fear of death to shape their every decision. But I have come to believe that the most profound way to live is to embrace our mortality to accept that death is a part of life, and that in acknowledging its presence, we are freed to live with greater clarity and purpose.

There is a strange paradox in our relationship with death. On one hand, we fear it because it represents the unknown, the end of everything we have come to know and love. Yet, on the other hand, it is the very thing that gives life its urgency, its meaning. If we were to live forever, what would compel us to make the most of our time? Mortality is what drives us to seek connection, to create, to love, and to leave a legacy. It is the ultimate reminder that every moment is precious and that we must not waste the time we are given.

In many ways, our awareness of mortality shapes the way we live our lives. We create goals, build relationships, and seek meaning, all in the context of knowing that we do not have forever. The impermanence of life pushes us to seek something lasting, something that will outlive us. Some turn to art or writing, leaving behind a record of their existence. Others invest in relationships, hoping that the love and kindness they give will ripple through generations. Still, others seek to make a difference in the world, contributing to causes that will continue long after they are gone. In these ways, we try to transcend our mortality, even as we acknowledge its inevitability. But what of the fear of death itself? It is a fear that resides deep within us, often unspoken but always present. We fear the loss of control, the cessation of consciousness, the fading of our identity. We fear leaving behind those we love, and the uncertainty of what if anything awaits us on the other side. For many, the fear of death is a driving force behind their actions, influencing decisions both large and small. Yet, as difficult as it is, confronting this fear head-on can lead to a profound shift in how we approach life.

    To face our mortality is to understand that life is fragile, and that control is an illusion. We do not know when our time will come, only that it will. This realization can be terrifying, but it can also be liberating. When we accept that death is a natural part of life, we can stop clinging so tightly to things that do not matter. We can release the need for perfection, for control, and instead focus on what truly matters: the experiences we create, the love we share, and the impact we leave behind.

In accepting our mortality, we also come to appreciate the present moment in a deeper way. Knowing that our days are numbered gives each moment a heightened significance. The simple act of watching a sunset, sharing a meal with loved ones, or feeling the warmth of the sun on our skin takes on a new level of meaning. These moments, which might otherwise pass unnoticed, become small treasures reminders of the beauty of life, even in its impermanence.

Mortality also teaches us about humility. It reminds us that we are not the center of the universe, that we are part of something much larger than ourselves. No matter how much we achieve or accumulate in life, death will come for us all. This humbling truth can help us put our egos in check, to see ourselves not as isolated individuals, but as interconnected beings, part of a larger human story. In this way, the awareness of death can inspire us to live with greater empathy and compassion, recognizing that the struggles and joys of life are shared by all.

Throughout history, different cultures and philosophies have offered their own perspectives on death and what lies beyond. For some, the promise of an afterlife offers comfort a belief that death is not the end, but a transition to something greater. For others, death is seen as the final end, with no consciousness beyond it. These differing beliefs shape how we view our mortality, influencing how we live and what we prioritize. Regardless of what we believe, the mystery of death remains. It is the ultimate unknown, and perhaps that is why it has such a profound hold on us.

The Stoics, in particular, believed that reflecting on death regularly was essential to living a virtuous life. They called this practice "memento mori" a reminder that we are mortal and that our time is limited. For the Stoics, death was not something to be feared, but something to be embraced as a natural part of the human experience. By keeping death in mind, they argued, we are better able to focus on what is within our control our actions, our character, and how we treat others. The rest, including the timing of our death, is beyond our control and therefore not worth worrying about.

This Stoic perspective offers a practical approach to mortality. Rather than allowing the fear of death to paralyze us, we can use it as motivation to live with intention and purpose. We can choose to spend our time wisely, to cultivate virtues like courage, compassion, and wisdom, knowing that these are the things that will endure long after we are gone. In this way, mortality becomes not a source of dread but a reminder to live fully and authentically. And yet, even with this philosophical perspective, the reality of death can still be overwhelming. It is one thing to reflect on mortality in the abstract, but quite another to face it in the context of losing someone we love. The death of a loved one brings our own mortality into sharp focus, forcing us to confront the fragility of life in the most personal way. Grief, in its rawest form, is a reminder of the deep connection we share with others, and the pain of loss is the price we pay for that connection.

In grieving, we honor the love we had, even as we are reminded of our own impermanence. But in the face of death, there is also resilience. Time and again, humanity has shown an incredible capacity to endure loss and continue on.

We find ways to honor the memory of those we have lost, to carry their spirit with us even after they are gone. In this way, death does not sever the bonds of love; it transforms them. The people we have lost remain a part of us, shaping who we are and how we live.

Ultimately, mortality is not something to be conquered or overcome. It is a fundamental aspect of what it means to be human. In acknowledging our mortality, we are reminded of the fleeting nature of life, but also of its beauty. We come to see that what matters most is not how long we live, but how fully we live. Mortality teaches us to cherish the present moment, to invest in relationships, and to pursue meaning, knowing that our time is limited.

In the end, the knowledge of our mortality can be a powerful guide. It asks us to live with urgency, but also with peace, accepting that we are part of the natural cycle of life and death. It invites us to make the most of our time, to leave the world a little better than we found it, and to face the unknown with courage.

Mortality is a companion we all know exists but rarely acknowledge until it demands our attention. For me, the presence of death has not been a distant, philosophical concept, but a recurring part of my journey. Losing friends and family members over the years has changed me in ways I never anticipated, reshaping my understanding of life's brevity and deepening my appreciation for the moments and connections we often take for granted.

The passing of my father was the first of many losses that would carve new perspectives into my life. His death was like a seismic shift, breaking apart my sense of invulnerability. It wasn't just that he was gone, but that something foundational had been taken away. I began to feel the weight of time, and for the first time, I truly grasped the idea that the people we love will not always be there. This realization made me more present, more aware of the way I spoke to others, the way I treated those around me. As more years passed, I saw friends, too, fade away—sometimes suddenly, and other times through a slow, aching journey. Each loss left behind its own kind of emptiness, its own lingering questions. Losing friends made me acutely aware of the fragility of youth. We often think that we have so much time, that we are immune to the tragedies that happen in other people's lives. But losing those friends reminded me that we are all walking the same uncertain path, where any moment could be our last.

The most painful part of loss is not the finality of death itself, but the countless moments that remain unlived. Conversations left unfinished, plans never seen through, and the dreams that once seemed so certain, all now suspended in a cruel limbo. I have learned that grief is not just about missing the person who is gone, but also mourning the life they were meant to continue living. It is a shadow that lingers over the future, altering how we envision the days ahead.

These experiences have changed me in a fundamental way. They have made me value authenticity in relationships. I no longer find comfort in surface-level connections; instead, I crave genuine conversations, moments that matter, and experiences that leave a mark on my heart. I've grown to understand that we are not promised tomorrow, and that realization has shifted how I prioritize my time and energy.

Through the passing of family members, I've come to see that our legacies are not in the achievements or accolades we accumulate, but in the memories and emotions we leave with others. My family's stories, the way they faced their own struggles and triumphs, and the love they gave so freely, continue to resonate within me. Their lives have become like beacons, reminding me of the values and lessons I hope to carry forward.

As I reflect on these losses, I am struck by the interconnectedness of life and death. Death is not an end, but a continuation of the human story, with each loss revealing new facets of love and resilience. There is a profound humility that comes with knowing that one day, I too will leave behind unfinished stories. This awareness has taught me to approach life with a greater sense of gratitude and urgency—to love more deeply, to forgive more readily, and to live more authentically.

One of the most significant changes I've noticed in myself is a new way of finding peace amidst uncertainty. There is no way to fully prepare for loss, but I've come to realize that the fear of death should not overshadow the joy of living. I've learned to hold onto moments more tightly—not out of desperation, but with an understanding that these fleeting glimpses of life are what give it its beauty. In embracing the uncertainty, I have found a new kind of freedom.

In all of this, I have come to see that mortality is not just a reminder of the end, but also of the beginning. It urges me to reflect on what kind of life I want to live and what kind of legacy I want to leave behind. These reflections have changed the way I set my goals, the way I treat others, and the way I view my own path. I've begun to measure life not by its length, but by the depth of its meaning.

The losses I've experienced have, paradoxically, given me a greater appreciation for life. They have taught me that while we cannot control when death arrives, we can choose how we live in the meantime. I am no longer afraid of mortality; rather, I see it as a call to live fully, to love fiercely, and to find purpose in each day. Through grief, I have found a deeper understanding of what it means to be alive. In the end, the knowledge of our mortality can be a powerful guide. It asks us to live with urgency, but also with peace, accepting that we are part of the natural cycle of life and death. It invites us to make the most of our time, to leave the world a little better than we found it, and to face the unknown with courage.

Reflections 6

Mortality,
a shadow that walks beside us,
silent and steady,
never far,
always present,
a reminder
that each breath
is borrowed.

We live as though we have
forever,
as though the days stretch on
without end,
but time,
like sand through open fingers,
slips away
before we realize it's gone.

There is a beauty in this
fragility,
in the way life blooms
for a moment,
then fades,

a flower in the sun
that wilts with the setting light.
We are not meant to last,
but in that brief existence,
we find meaning.

Mortality humbles us,
makes us remember
that we are not infinite,
that our bodies will one day
return to the earth,
dust to dust,
ash to ash. But the spirit, the
spark, lives on in ways we cannot
see.
Each heartbeat is a countdown,
a rhythm to the dance
we do with time.
And yet,
it is this very ending
that gives life its urgency,
its sweetness.
Without death,
would we cherish the moments
that flicker and fade?
Would we grasp so tightly

to love,
to joy,
to hope?

Mortality is not an enemy,
but a companion
a reminder
that we are here,
alive,
for this fleeting moment
in the vastness of eternity.
It asks us to look at our days
with open eyes,
to feel the weight of each second
as it passes,
to live fully
while we can.

We fear it,
try to push it away,
but death,
like sleep,
comes for us all,
a final rest
after the long journey
of being.

And in that rest,
perhaps there is peace,
a return to the quiet
from which we came.

What matters,
in the end,
is not the length of days
but the depth of living,
the connections we make,
the love we give
without measure.
For when we are gone,
it is not the things we owned
that remain,
but the echoes of our kindness,
the ripples of our presence
in the lives of those we touched.

Mortality,
a shadow,
but also, a light
for in knowing we will end,
we find the courage to begin.

Purpose and Destiny

Purpose and destiny, often used interchangeably, yet fundamentally distinct. Purpose speaks to the reason behind our existence, the "why" that gives our life meaning. Destiny, on the other hand, refers to what we are meant to become, the path that life has laid out for us. While purpose is something we actively seek, destiny often feels like something that seeks us. To grapple with these two ideas is to grapple with the core of our existence: why are we here, and where are we headed?

For much of life, the search for purpose feels like an endless quest. We try to find meaning in careers, relationships, passions, and accomplishments, yet we often find that none of these fully satisfy the deeper longing within us. Purpose, it seems, is not something that can be easily defined or discovered. It requires introspection, patience, and a willingness to live with uncertainty. Often, we don't realize our purpose until we have lived through a series of experiences, some joyful, others painful. Purpose, in many ways, reveals itself through the journey.

In my own life, there have been moments when I thought I understood my purpose only to realize later that what I had thought was the ultimate goal was merely a steppingstone. This is the paradox of purpose: it is both something we discover and something we create. We may begin life thinking that our purpose is tied to a particular job or role, but as we grow and change, so too does our understanding of what we are meant to do. Our purpose evolves as we evolve, shaped by the experiences we encounter along the way.

There was a time when I believed that success, as defined by society career accomplishments, financial stability, recognition was the key to purpose. But with time, I realized that these external markers, while important, could not fill the deeper void within. I found myself asking: what is the point of all this achievement if it doesn't bring fulfillment? This realization marked a turning point for me, where I began to seek purpose not in what I could accomplish, but in how I could contribute to something greater than myself.

Destiny, on the other hand, has always felt like a more mysterious force something that pulls us in directions we cannot fully understand or predict. While purpose is something we can shape with our choices, destiny often feels like a path that is laid before us, whether we realize it or not. There have been moments in my life when I felt an inexplicable pull toward a particular direction, even when it made no logical sense. These moments of intuition, of feeling guided by something beyond myself, have often led to the most meaningful experiences of my life.

I think of destiny as the thread that runs through our lives, connecting seemingly unrelated events and decisions. At the time, we may not see the significance of these moments, but as the years pass, we begin to notice patterns, connections, and synchronicities. It is only in hindsight that we can begin to see how the choices we made, the people we met, and the challenges we faced were all part of a larger design. Destiny, in this sense, is not something that is imposed upon us, but something that unfolds through the choices we make.

There have been times in my life when I resisted the path that seemed to be laid out for me. I clung to what I thought I wanted, only to find that life had other plans. At first, I saw these detours as failures or setbacks, but as time went on, I began to realize that these so-called failures were guiding me toward something more aligned with my true purpose. Destiny, I have come to believe, is not about achieving a specific goal or reaching a predetermined endpoint. It is about becoming the person we are meant to be, through the lessons we learn along the way.

One example from my own life comes to mind when I think of purpose and destiny intertwining. I had always envisioned a certain career path for myself one that was stable, respected, and aligned with societal expectations. I worked hard to achieve success in this field, pouring years of effort into building a career that I believed would define me. Yet, despite my achievements, I felt a growing sense of emptiness. It was as if the more I accomplished, the further I drifted from my true self.

It wasn't until a series of unexpected life events some painful, others illuminating that I began to question this path. These events forced me to step back and reevaluate what truly mattered to me. In doing so, I realized that my purpose was not tied to a specific job or title, but to a deeper calling: to help others, to connect, and to create something meaningful. This realization didn't come all at once; it unfolded slowly, through moments of doubt, reflection, and a willingness to let go of what I thought my life should look like.

Destiny often works in this way, guiding us through a process of shedding the superficial layers of identity we've constructed, revealing something truer underneath. It is rarely a straightforward path, and it almost never looks like what we imagined. But if we are open to it, destiny has a way of leading us to exactly where we need to be, even if the journey is winding and difficult.

One of the most profound lessons I've learned is that purpose and destiny are not about finding a singular, fixed path. Instead, they are about embracing the process of becoming. We are constantly evolving, and with each new phase of life, our sense of purpose and our understanding of destiny deepen. We are not bound to the choices we made in the past; we are free to grow, to change direction, and to redefine what a meaningful life looks like.

There is a certain freedom in this realization, knowing that purpose and destiny are not rigid, but fluid. It allows us to approach life with curiosity, rather than fear. Instead of trying to control every outcome or predict every twist in the road, we can trust that even when things don't go according to plan, they are still part of the unfolding of our destiny. Every experience, whether joyful or painful, is a stepping stone toward greater understanding and growth.

In moments of doubt or uncertainty, I have often reminded myself that purpose is not something we achieve once and for all. It is something we must continually cultivate, refine, and rediscover. Destiny, too, is not a fixed endpoint, but a journey a journey that is shaped by the choices we make and the lessons we learn. The two are intertwined, guiding us toward a deeper understanding of who we are and what we are meant to contribute to the world.

Purpose and destiny are ultimately about alignment about living in a way that is true to ourselves and in harmony with the larger forces at play in our lives. When we are in alignment, we feel a sense of flow, of being exactly where we are meant to be. But this alignment is not something we achieve once and hold onto forever. It is something we must continually work toward, through moments of clarity and moments of confusion.

As I reflect on my own journey, I see that my purpose and destiny have been shaped not by the things I have achieved, but by the challenges I have faced, the relationships I have built, and the ways in which I have responded to the unexpected twists in the road. In the end, it is not about reaching a particular destination, but about how we walk the path how we choose to show up in the world, moment by moment.

To live with purpose is to live with intention, to seek meaning in the everyday. To embrace destiny is to trust in the unfolding of life, to have faith that even when the path is unclear, we are being guided toward something greater. The two are not separate, but deeply intertwined, leading us toward a life of fulfillment, growth, and contribution.

Reflections 7

Purpose,
a quiet whisper
in the stillness of our hearts,
a call that stirs beneath the
surface,
waiting for us to listen,
to follow where it leads,
even when the path is unclear.

We search for it,
in the spaces between our days,
in the work we do,
in the faces of those we love.
It hides sometimes,
just beyond reach,
but we feel its pull,
a magnet drawing us
toward something greater
than ourselves.

Destiny,
a word heavy with meaning,
yet elusive.
Is it written in the stars,
etched into the fabric of time?
Or is it shaped by our choices,
by the steps we take
into the unknown?

We walk between purpose and
destiny,
each decision a thread
weaving into a tapestry
we cannot fully see.
And yet,
there is a sense
that we are guided,
that something larger moves us
toward where we are meant to
be.

Sometimes, purpose feels clear
a light we follow
without question,
a knowing that fills our days
with meaning.

Other times,
it fades,
lost in the noise of the world,
and we wander,
unsure of which way to turn.

But even in the wandering,
there is a purpose
a lesson,
a truth to be uncovered
in the uncertainty,
in the waiting.
For destiny is not a straight line,
but a winding road,
full of detours,
twists,
and unexpected turns.

We are the authors
of our own stories,
and yet,
there are moments
that feel destined
as if the universe
has conspired
to bring us to a place
we were always meant to be.

Purpose is the reason we rise,
the force that drives us forward,
even when the way is hard,
even when doubt clouds our
minds.
It is the fuel
for the fire inside us,
the spark that ignites
when we realize
we are here for a reason.
Destiny waits,
patient and still,
like a river's current,
carrying us along,
sometimes gently,
sometimes with force,

but always toward something,
something we cannot yet name.

In the end,
purpose and destiny dance
together,
a rhythm that moves through us,
carving out the shape
of whom we are meant to
become.
And though we may not always
see it,
we are exactly where we need to
be,
each moment a step
on the journey toward ourselves.

The Harmony of All Things

There is a quiet, profound truth in the realization that everything in life is connected—that beneath the surface chaos of existence lies an intricate harmony binding all things together. From the vast expanses of the cosmos to the smallest details of everyday life, this harmony is ever-present, weaving through the fabric of our experiences. The more deeply we reflect on the world around us, the more we begin to see that nothing exists in isolation. Each event, each thought, each movement is part of a larger, cosmic rhythm.

Harmony in life doesn't mean the absence of conflict or disorder. In fact, it often arises from the balance of opposites light and dark, joy and sorrow, creation and destruction. These dualities coexist, constantly shifting and evolving, giving rise to the complexity of life itself. Like the interplay of musical notes in a symphony, the contrasts are what make the whole experience rich and meaningful. Without dissonance, there can be no resolution, and without chaos, there can be no understanding of peace. In this way, the very imperfections we encounter are essential components of a greater order.

Think of nature, where we can observe this harmony most clearly. The seasons change, each with its distinct character, yet together they create a cycle that sustains life. The leaves fall from the trees in autumn, decay in winter, and nourish new growth in spring. There is beauty in every phase of this process, even in death, which is itself part of the continuum of life. The trees do not resist the coming of winter, nor do the flowers struggle against the warmth of the sun. They accept the cycles as they come, flowing with the rhythm of the universe.

As humans, however, we often resist the natural flow of life. We cling to permanence, grasping for control in a world that is constantly changing. We want to hold onto moments of happiness, fearing that their loss will bring us pain, but in doing so, we disrupt the natural harmony. Like a river that is dammed, our resistance creates stagnation. Life, in its essence, is fluid. It moves, shifts, and transforms, and to find true peace, we must learn to move with it rather than against it.

At the core of harmony lies acceptance, the ability to embrace life as it is, not as we wish it to be. This doesn't mean passivity or resignation but rather a deep understanding that every experience, whether joyful or painful, has a place in the larger order of things. When we accept life's imperfections, we begin to see that each moment, no matter how small or seemingly insignificant, is part of a greater whole. The sorrow we feel in one season may give rise to wisdom in another. The struggles we face today may be the seeds of strength tomorrow.

This understanding of harmony can also be applied to our relationships. Just as in nature, human connections are complex, dynamic, and often unpredictable. There will be moments of deep connection and moments of misunderstanding, times of closeness and times of distance. But if we view our relationships as part of a larger harmony, we can approach them with greater patience and compassion. We begin to see that conflict, too, is part of the dance, necessary for growth and deeper understanding. It is not something to be feared or avoided but embraced as part of the process.

In the broader scope of the universe, we are reminded of our smallness, yet simultaneously, our connection to everything. The stars, burning millions of light-years away, are made of the same elements that course through our veins. The air we breathe is shared by all living things, the same molecules cycling through time and space, connecting us to the past and the future. In this sense, we are never truly alone. We are part of a vast, interconnected web of life that stretches beyond our comprehension, and to live in harmony is to recognize our place within this web.

Even within ourselves, there is a delicate balance that must be maintained. Our minds, bodies, and spirits are in constant dialogue, each influencing the other. When we neglect one aspect of our being, the others suffer. To live harmoniously, we must nurture all parts of ourselves, honoring the physical, emotional, and spiritual dimensions of our existence. Just as a garden needs water, sunlight, and care to thrive, so too do we need attention, reflection, and nourishment to maintain our inner balance.

Harmony, then, is not something we achieve once and for all; it is a practice, a way of being that requires ongoing awareness and adjustment. Life will inevitably throw us out of balance through loss, change, or unforeseen challenges but if we approach these moments with an understanding of the larger harmony, we can find our way back. It is in these times of imbalance that we have the opportunity to grow, to learn more about ourselves and the world around us. The process of returning to harmony is itself an essential part of life's rhythm.

Consider the practice of mindfulness, which teaches us to be present with whatever is happening in the moment. When we are mindful, we tune into the natural harmony of life, noticing the ebb and flow of our thoughts, emotions, and sensations without judgment. We observe how everything is in constant motion, how nothing remains the same, and in this observation, we find peace. We come to realize that harmony is not about forcing things to be a certain way but about allowing them to unfold naturally.

Even in moments of great pain or suffering, harmony can be found. These experiences, difficult as they may be, are part of the fabric of life. Pain teaches us, shapes us, and ultimately deepens our capacity for empathy and compassion. In the grander scheme, even suffering has its place. It humbles us, reminding us of our vulnerability and our need for one another. Through the experience of suffering, we come to understand the interconnectedness of all beings, how our actions and choices ripple through the lives of others, influencing the world in ways we may never fully see.

There is also a harmony in time itself. Past, present, and future are not separate entities but flow together in an unbroken stream. The choices we make today are influenced by our past, and they will shape our future. Yet, the only moment we truly have is the present, and it is here that we can touch the fullness of life. When we live in harmony with time, we do not dwell in the regrets of the past or anxieties about the future. Instead, we immerse ourselves fully in the now, trusting that the flow of time will carry us where we need to go.

Harmony, then, is both an individual and a collective experience. It requires us to find balance within ourselves, but it also asks us to recognize our role in the larger community of life. When we live in harmony with others, we act with kindness, understanding that our well-being is tied to the well-being of those around us. We become stewards of the earth, caretakers of our relationships, and, most importantly, mindful participants in the unfolding of life.

In this way, harmony is not a distant ideal or an abstract concept. It is something we can cultivate in our daily lives through the way we treat others, the way we care for the earth, and the way we respond to the challenges and joys that come our way. It is an ongoing practice, a dance with life that requires both flexibility and awareness.

The more we embrace this practice, the more we realize that harmony is not something we need to seek it is already here, waiting for us to recognize it. The harmony of all things reminds us that we are part of something much larger than ourselves. Our lives, with all their complexities, are threads in the great tapestry of existence. To live in harmony is to honor that interconnectedness, to embrace the flow of life with grace and humility. It is to recognize that we are both small and significant, fleeting and eternal, and that within the rhythm of all things, we are exactly where we need to be.

Reflections 8

There is a thread,
invisible,
that ties us all together
a rhythm,
a pulse
beneath the noise of the world,
where all things move
in quiet harmony.

The wind whispers to the trees,
the trees to the earth,
the earth to the rivers
that carve their way
through stone and time.
Everything speaks,
in a language older than words,
a language of being.

We are part of it,
though we forget,
wrapped in our small concerns,
our minds busy with plans
and the rush of days.

But even when we forget,
the harmony holds us,
a silent song
that hums beneath our feet.

The stars above us
burn in patterns
older than memory,
casting their light
into the same sky
our ancestors gazed upon,
their stories etched in the
constellations,
their voices still echoing
in the dark.

Each moment is woven
into the fabric of existence,
each breath part of a cycle
that began before we were born
and will continue long after we
are gone.
The seasons turn,
the tides rise and fall,
and we,
we are caught in the same current,

moving with the tides
whether we know it or not.

The birds sing in the morning
light,
the sun rises,
and for a moment,
everything is still,
everything in its place,
as if the universe itself
is taking a breath,
holding it
before releasing us once more
into the flow.

In this harmony,
there is no separation,
only connection.
The waves crash on distant
shores,
and somewhere,
we feel it
a tug,
a pull,
a reminder that we are not alone
in this vast, spinning world.

The atoms that make us
were born in the heart of stars,
scattered across galaxies,
and now they sing in our bones,
a testament to the truth
that we are made of the same stuff
as the universe itself.
There is harmony
in the way life moves in the
dance of birth and death,
in the quiet moments of joy,
in the deep wells of sorrow.
It is all part of the same song,
a melody that rises and falls,
but never breaks.

We touch the earth
and it holds us,
gives us life,
and in return,
we breathe out what it needs,
a perfect exchange,
a cycle that continues
even when we are unaware.

In the harmony of all things,
there is peace.
Not the absence of pain,
but a deeper knowing
that all is as it should be,
that the rivers will always find
the
sea,
and the stars will continue to
burn
long after we are gone.

We are part of this symphony,
our lives a single note
in the vast song of creation.
And though we may not always
hear
it,
the harmony holds,
binding us to each other,
to the earth,
to the stars,
and to all that is.

In this harmony,
we find our place
not apart,
but within,
woven into the fabric
of everything that ever was
and ever will be.
We are the song,
and we are the silence that
follows.

Freedom and Acceptance

Freedom and acceptance are two sides of a deeply intertwined coin. At first glance, they might seem to pull us in different directions: freedom often suggests an unshackled state, a life lived without constraints, while acceptance implies yielding, a surrender to what is. Yet, the more we reflect on their relationship, the more we realize that true freedom is found through acceptance, not in resistance. It is in accepting the things we cannot change, the limitations of our circumstances, and the truths of our existence that we begin to experience a deeper sense of liberation.

Freedom is not simply the absence of boundaries. We may long for a life where we are free from obligations, free from pain, free from the expectations placed upon us by society or others, but such a life is a mirage. To be human is to be bound by certain limitations time, mortality, the unpredictability of life. These are facts we cannot escape. If we spend our energy fighting against these truths, we only trap ourselves in a cycle of frustration and dissatisfaction. True freedom, then, is not about removing limitations but about learning to live in harmony with them.

Acceptance, on the other hand, is often misunderstood as passivity or resignation. It's easy to think that accepting our circumstances means giving up, but acceptance is not about surrendering our agency. It is about recognizing reality as it is, not as we wish it to be. In doing so, we free ourselves from the struggle against what cannot be controlled. Acceptance is a form of courage it requires us to face life with open eyes, to acknowledge both the beauty and the pain, the certainty and the uncertainty, and to find peace within that awareness.

In my own life, there have been countless moments where I struggled against reality, wanting things to be different than they were. I would cling to ideals or fantasies of how my life should unfold, and when things inevitably didn't go according to plan, I felt trapped by disappointment, regret, or anger. Yet, the more I tried to exert control over life's uncontrollable elements, the more I found myself bound by those very things. It was only when I began to practice acceptance accepting the imperfection of my own plans, accepting that life was always going to surprise me that I started to feel a sense of freedom emerge.

Freedom through acceptance doesn't mean that we give up on change or growth. Quite the opposite. It is through accepting the present moment as it is that we become free to take meaningful action. When we stop resisting what is and instead focus on what we can influence, we are empowered to move forward in a way that aligns with reality rather than against it. Acceptance creates space for clarity, and with clarity comes the ability to make conscious choices. The path forward becomes clearer, not because we've controlled the world around us, but because we've aligned ourselves with it.

One of the greatest areas where acceptance leads to freedom is in our relationships. Often, we enter relationships with expectations of how others should act, how they should meet our needs, or how they should change to fit our ideals. But people, like life itself, are unpredictable and imperfect. When we cling to rigid expectations of others, we only set ourselves up for frustration and conflict. True freedom in relationships comes from accepting others as they are, with their flaws, their strengths, and their humanity. In doing so, we free ourselves from the need to control or fix, and instead, we allow love and connection to flourish in its most authentic form.

Acceptance also frees us from the burden of self-judgment. We live in a world that constantly tells us we should be more successful, more attractive, more accomplished. We internalize these messages and often become our harshest critics. Yet, the freedom to be ourselves, to embrace our imperfections and limitations, can only come through self-acceptance. This doesn't mean we stop striving to grow or improve, but it does mean that we approach ourselves with kindness and understanding rather than judgment and criticism. In accepting ourselves, we become free from the need to prove our worth to others or even to ourselves

The greatest freedom of all, perhaps, comes in accepting the unknown. Life is full of uncertainty. We don't know what tomorrow holds, and we can never fully predict or control the future. This uncertainty can be a source of great fear, but it can also be a source of liberation. When we accept that uncertainty is a natural part of existence, we no longer feel the need to grip so tightly to the illusion of control. Instead, we can live fully in the present, appreciating each moment for what it is rather than constantly worrying about what might come next.

There is a quiet, powerful freedom in accepting the impermanence of life. We are all passing through this world for a brief moment, and nothing we experience whether joy or pain will last forever. When we accept this truth, we stop holding onto experiences or identities that no longer serve us. We become free to let go, to evolve, to live lightly, knowing that every moment is fleeting and precious. Acceptance of impermanence frees us to live with more presence, more openness, and more gratitude.

In the end, freedom and acceptance are not separate; they are deeply connected. To be truly free is to live in alignment with reality, to accept the things we cannot change, and to focus our energy on the things we can. This is not an easy path, it requires humility, patience, and trust but it is a path that leads to peace. By accepting life as it is, we discover a freedom that is not dependent on external circumstances but rooted in a deep inner resilience. It is a freedom that allows us to live fully, authentically, and without fear.

Reflections 9

Freedom,
that elusive breath of air,
that open sky stretching wide
beyond the cages we build,
beyond the walls of expectation
and the chains of what could be.
It whispers to us in moments of
quiet,
when the weight of the world
lifts,
even for just a second.

We chase it,
thinking it's something to be
won,
something to be fought for
and claimed,
a distant shore
that if we swim hard enough,
fast enough,
we might just reach.

But freedom is not out there,
not on the horizon
or in the breaking of chains.
It lives within,
in the spaces we surrender,
in the gentle letting go
of what we cannot hold.
It is not the absence of
boundaries
but the peace that comes
from knowing who we are
and where we stand.

Acceptance is its quiet twin,
the soft sigh of surrender,
the release of what we thought
we needed to be.
It's the quieting of the inner
storm,
the embrace of the imperfect,
the recognition that this moment,
just as it is, is enough.
We spend our lives seeking
freedom
from our fears,

our pasts,
the parts of ourselves
we wish were different.
But true freedom is not found
in the escape,
but in the return
the return to ourselves,
to the messy, beautiful truth
of whom we are.

Acceptance doesn't ask us to
change,
to strive,
to become someone else.
It asks us to sit with what is,
to be still in the discomfort,
to see the shadows
and the light
and call them both our own.

It is in this acceptance
that freedom blooms,
like a flower in the cracks of
stone,
defiant and delicate,
strong not in spite of its fragility

but because of it.
To accept is to free ourselves
from the need to be perfect, to be
anything other than human.
Freedom is not the soaring
flight,
but the quiet courage
to stand in our truth,
to let go of the masks
we've worn for too long,
to show up as we are
and say,
"Here I am."

It is found in the breath we take
when we forgive ourselves,
when we let the past rest,
when we unclench our hands
from the reins
and let life
unfold.

Acceptance is the doorway,
the open gate
through which freedom walks.
It is the softening of the heart,
the unclenching of the fist,
the gentle nod to the self
that says,
"You are enough."

In the end,
freedom and acceptance are not
separate,
but the same path
walked in different ways.
To be free is to accept,
and to accept is to be free,
both bound by the same truth
that we are here,
in this moment,
whole and unfinished,
fragile and strong, perfect in our
imperfection.
And so, we breathe,
we let go,
we surrender
to the ebb and flow of life,

knowing that in this dance
of freedom and acceptance,
we find not just ourselves
but the world,
wide and waiting,
open and endless.

Wisdom and Inner Peace

Wisdom and inner peace are often seen as lofty ideals, unattainable unless we remove ourselves from the world's complexities. But true wisdom and inner peace are not about escape they are about learning to navigate the storm while remaining centered. They come from within, nurtured through self-awareness, acceptance, and the understanding that life, in its ever-changing nature, offers no guarantees. To find wisdom and inner peace is to realize that the calm we seek outside of ourselves can only be cultivated within.

Wisdom is often born out of our willingness to sit with discomfort. It's easy to think that peace can only be found when everything is in order when there is no chaos, no conflict, no pain. But life is rarely so simple. Inner peace does not mean a life free from difficulty; rather, it is the ability to remain grounded in the face of life's inevitable challenges. Wisdom helps us see that peace is not the absence of difficulty but the presence of an inner stillness that can withstand it.

In my own life, I've come to realize that moments of wisdom often emerge not in times of ease but in times of struggle. It is in facing hardship that we learn the most about ourselves, and it is through hardship that we cultivate resilience. Inner peace is not something that is given; it is earned through experience, through learning how to let go of what we cannot control and focus on what we can. This process takes time, patience, and a deep willingness to accept the messiness of life.

One of the hardest lessons in the pursuit of wisdom and inner peace is learning how to let go of expectations, of the need for control, of the idea that we can shape life into exactly what we want it to be. So much of our suffering comes from resisting the natural flow of life, from clinging to the belief that things should be different than they are. Wisdom teaches us that peace can only be found in acceptance, in releasing our grip on what we think should happen and learning to embrace what is happening.

There is a certain quiet wisdom in understanding that we cannot always force solutions. Often, the more we try to control outcomes, the more entangled we become in the very problems we are trying to solve. Inner peace comes from stepping back, from allowing space for things to unfold naturally. It's in these moments of surrender that wisdom reveals itself, not in the form of a grand epiphany but as a gentle, steady reminder that life's unfolding is often wiser than our attempts to direct it.

Inner peace is also deeply connected to self-compassion. So many of us are in constant battle with ourselves, endlessly striving for perfection or for some version of success that we think will bring us happiness. But wisdom teaches us that inner peace cannot be found in the future or in achieving some external goal. It is found here, in the present moment, when we accept ourselves fully, with all our flaws and imperfections. It is in this acceptance that we begin to experience a deeper, more authentic sense of peace.

To cultivate inner peace, we must also learn to quiet the mind. Our minds are often restless, filled with thoughts, worries, and judgments that pull us away from the present. Wisdom teaches us to recognize these mental distractions for what they are impermanent and often irrelevant. Inner peace comes when we learn to observe our thoughts without attaching to them, when we can let them pass like clouds in the sky, knowing that they do not define us or our experience.

There is a profound wisdom in understanding that life is transient. Everything we experience joy, pain, success, failure is temporary. This realization is not meant to make us feel hopeless but to free us from the burden of taking life too seriously. Inner peace arises when we understand that nothing lasts forever and that, in this impermanence, there is beauty. We can let go of the need to hold onto every experience, knowing that life is in constant motion, and peace is found in flowing with it rather than resisting it.

In relationships, wisdom and inner peace teach us the value of presence and acceptance. We often place expectations on others, hoping they will fulfill our needs or live up to certain ideals. But true wisdom in relationships comes from letting go of these expectations and accepting others as they are. Inner peace flourishes when we stop trying to change or control those around us and instead focus on being fully present, compassionate, and understanding.

Another key aspect of wisdom and inner peace is learning to live in alignment with our values. So much of the discontent we experience comes from living in ways that are disconnected from who we truly are. Wisdom helps us recognize this misalignment, and inner peace is the reward for making choices that honor our deepest values and truths. It's in living authentically, even when it's difficult, that we find a profound sense of peace and contentment.

Inner peace also involves embracing uncertainty. Life is inherently unpredictable, and wisdom comes from accepting that we cannot know what the future holds. Rather than being paralyzed by fear of the unknown, inner peace encourages us to trust the process of life, to trust that even in uncertainty, we can find stability within ourselves. This kind of trust is not easy to cultivate, but it is essential for living with a sense of peace that is not dependent on external circumstances.

Ultimately, wisdom and inner peace are deeply intertwined. Wisdom guides us to recognize that inner peace is not something we acquire but something we uncover within ourselves. It is always there, waiting beneath the noise of our thoughts, our worries, and our desires. Through introspection, mindfulness, and acceptance, we learn to access that peace and let it guide us through life's inevitable ups and downs.

In the end, wisdom is not about knowing everything or having all the answers. It is about knowing ourselves, accepting the world as it is, and finding peace in the knowledge that, while we cannot control everything, we can always choose how we respond. Inner peace is not a destination but a state of being one that is cultivated through patience, practice, and a deep, compassionate understanding of the world and ourselves.

Reflections 10

Wisdom comes softly,
not as a shout,
but as a whisper
carried on the wind,
a quiet knowing
that settles in the heart
like the calm after a storm.
It is not found in answers,
but in the acceptance
that some questions
have none.
We spend our days searching,
chasing truths
like leaves in the breeze,
thinking that wisdom
is something to be caught,
to be held,
to be owned.
But wisdom is not a prize
it is the slow unfolding
of understanding,
the gentle release
of what we thought we knew.

Inner peace,
that elusive stillness,
is the soft echo of wisdom's
touch,
a resting place
in the chaos of living.
It is not the absence of noise,
but the quiet center
we carry within,
a sanctuary of breath and being.
In the rush of the world,
we often lose it
that thread of calm
that weaves through the
moments
of our days.
We get caught in the swirl
of doing,
of striving,
of becoming more
than we already are.
But wisdom reminds us
to pause,
to breathe,
to find the silence
that sits patiently beneath it all.

Peace is not a destination,
not a mountain to be climbed
or a treasure to be found.
It is the soft exhale
when we let go of striving,
when we stop trying to be
anything other
than who we are
right now.

Wisdom teaches us
that life is not about control,
not about bending the world
to our will,
but about flowing with the
currents,
trusting the river
to carry us
where we are meant to go.
It is the surrender
to the present,
the letting go of the need to know
what comes next.
There is a peace
that comes
when we embrace the unknown,

when we see that uncertainty
is not a threat,
but a canvas
blank and open, waiting for the
brushstrokes
of our choices.
Inner peace is the quiet friend
of wisdom,
the still lake
reflecting the sky,
unmoved by the ripples
that dance on its surface.
It does not seek
to change the world,
but to change the way
we see it
to soften our gaze,
to open our hearts,
to rest in the truth
that we are enough,
even in our unknowing.

In the end,
wisdom and peace are not found
in the distant reaches of thought,

but in the simple moments
in the pause before speaking,
in the breath between actions,
in the quiet acceptance
of what is.
They are the gentle hands
that hold us steady
when the winds of life
blow strong,
the quiet voice that says, "Be
still. You are where you need to
be."
And in that stillness,
we find the peace
that has been there all along,
the wisdom that rises
not from the mind,
but from the heart
a quiet truth that needs no proof,
only the soft, steady beat of being.

Gratitude and the Gift of Life

Gratitude is one of the most powerful forces we can cultivate within ourselves. It's a lens through which the world changes, not externally but from within. When we are truly grateful, the simplest things a sunrise, the breath in our lungs, the warmth of another's presence become treasures. Yet, in the rush and complexity of life, it is easy to forget how miraculous it is to simply be alive. The gift of life, in its fragility and fleetingness, is a constant reminder that everything we experience is a privilege, even the difficult moments.

    Gratitude, however, is not always an instinctive response. Often, we take for granted what we have until it is lost. We forget the significance of the ordinary because we are so accustomed to it. The ability to walk, to think, to feel joy, to grieve these are things we overlook in the everyday shuffle of tasks and responsibilities. But wisdom reveals that nothing in life is guaranteed. Every breath we take is a miracle, and recognizing this transforms our entire experience of living.

There have been many moments in my life where I found myself lost in a cycle of dissatisfaction, longing for more, or wishing circumstances were different. It is in these times that gratitude feels the furthest away. Yet, it is precisely during such moments that the practice of gratitude becomes most essential. By intentionally shifting focus from what we lack to what we have, a profound shift takes place. Gratitude doesn't deny the existence of challenges but instead broadens our perspective, allowing us to see the beauty in what remains amidst the struggle.

Life itself is a gift, though we often forget this truth as we move through our routines. We expect tomorrow to come, and the days to unfold much like the ones before them. But life is fragile and unpredictable. Gratitude teaches us to cherish each moment, not because it will last forever, but because it won't. The fleeting nature of time gives every experience, every interaction, every breath a significance that is easy to overlook. In embracing gratitude, we begin to see life not as something owed to us but as a blessing.

One of the greatest challenges to living a life of gratitude is our tendency to focus on what we don't have. Our culture often encourages comparison, driving us to seek more and more, whether in terms of material possessions, success, or even happiness. But gratitude is not about having everything; it's about recognizing the value of what we already have. It asks us to stop chasing an idealized version of life and instead appreciate the present moment for what it is imperfect, yes, but filled with beauty, nonetheless.

In my own life, there have been times when the weight of what I didn't have seemed overwhelming when goals were unmet, or relationships fell short of my expectations. In those moments, it was gratitude that eventually brought me back to center. By focusing on the blessings that were present the people who supported me, the lessons I was learning, the small joys that persisted I was able to shift my perspective. This shift didn't erase the pain or difficulty, but it allowed me to move through them with more grace and acceptance.

Gratitude opens the heart. It allows us to connect more deeply with others, to see their humanity, and to acknowledge the role they play in our own journey.

Often, we move through life so quickly that we fail to fully appreciate the people who touch our lives, whether in big ways or small. Gratitude reminds us to pause, to express thanks, to recognize that none of us moves through life entirely alone. Every connection, no matter how fleeting, is part of the larger gift of life.

There is also a deep sense of peace that comes with gratitude. When we are focused on what we don't have or what might go wrong, anxiety and restlessness can take hold. But when we turn our attention to what is good, what is present, what is enough, a calmness settles within us. Gratitude anchors us in the here and now, freeing us from the endless cycle of wanting and waiting for something more. It reminds us that this moment, just as it is, holds its own perfection.

Reflections 11

Life,
a fragile miracle,
a flicker of light
in the vast expanse of time,
each moment a gift
wrapped in the quiet beat
of our hearts.
We wake each day
to the soft promise of morning,
to the sun that rises
without asking
if we are ready.

Gratitude is the breath we take
when we pause,
when we look around
and truly see
the beauty of the ordinary
the warmth of sunlight
through a window,
the sound of laughter
drifting on the air,
the gentle touch of a hand
that says,

"I am here."
How easy it is
to forget these gifts,
to rush past the wonder
of simply being.
We move so quickly,
our minds busy with the next
thing,
the next place,
the next moment, forgetting that
this one, right here, is enough.
Gratitude is the quiet shift,
the softening of the gaze
that sees not what is missing,
but what is here
the steady breath,
the beating heart,
the body that carries us
through each day,
despite the wear and tear
of living.
Life is a series of small wonders,
tiny miracles
that unfold without fanfare
the bloom of a flower
on a city sidewalk,

the way the sky shifts
from blue to gold
at the end of a long day,
the comforting rhythm
of a familiar song.

In gratitude,
we find the space
to truly live,
to be present
in the moments that matter,
to hold the people, we love
a little closer,
to speak the words
we often leave unsaid.
It is the thread
that connects us
to the deeper currents
of our own hearts,
to the quiet knowing
that we are part of something
greater than ourselves.

Gratitude turns the mundane
into the magical,
the routine

into the sacred.
It is the lens
that transforms the ordinary
into a celebration,
a reminder that every breath
is a new beginning,
every heartbeat
a gift.

And when we face the dark
days,
the heavy moments
that weigh on our spirit,
gratitude is the hand
that lifts us,
the light that shines
through the cracks.
It does not erase the pain,
but it helps us find the beauty
that remains.
We are here,
alive in this fleeting moment,
part of the great dance
of existence.
And that,
in all its imperfection,

is enough.
To be alive,
to feel,
to love,
to hope
these are the gifts
that life gives freely,
if only we choose to see them.
So let us live
with open hearts,
with eyes that see the beauty
in the everyday,
with hands that reach out
in kindness.
Let us give thanks
not just for the big moments,
but for the small ones,
the quiet joys
that fill our days.
For life is a gift,
precious and brief,
and gratitude
is the song we sing
to honor it,
a hymn of thanks
for all that is,

all that has been,
and all that is yet to come.

May we carry it with us,
this quiet knowing,
this gentle grace,
and may it guide us
through the days
with a heart full of wonder,
a spirit that sees the light
in every shadow,
and a soul
that knows
the profound beauty
of being.

Solitude and Connection

Solitude and connection are two seemingly opposing forces, yet they exist in an intricate dance within each of us. To be alone is often seen as something to be avoided, a space filled with emptiness or isolation. And connection especially in today's world is often idealized as the pinnacle of human experience, the point at which we are most fulfilled. But true connection cannot exist without a deep understanding of solitude, and solitude, when embraced, leads to richer, more meaningful connections. In this balance, we discover that the silence of solitude and the warmth of connection are not opposites; they are two sides of the same coin, each nurturing the other.

Solitude, for many, is uncomfortable. The quiet that accompanies it can feel deafening, filled with thoughts that we typically drown out through distraction. Yet, solitude, when approached not as something to escape but as something to embrace, becomes an opportunity for self-discovery. It is in those moments when we are most alone that we are also closest to ourselves. The noise of the external world fades, and we are left with the quiet of our own being. This can be daunting, but it is also where the seeds of wisdom are planted.

There is a profound depth to be found in solitude, a depth that often eludes us in the constant interaction and busyness of life. Solitude allows us to explore the corners of our minds that we tend to ignore or avoid. In solitude, we are faced with our thoughts, emotions, fears, and desires in their rawest forms. It is here, in the stillness, that we can begin to understand who we truly are beneath the layers of societal expectations and the roles we play for others. Solitude strips away the external and leaves us with the internal a confrontation with the self that is both challenging and transformative.

Yet, this confrontation with the self is not a form of isolation or loneliness. Rather, it is a space for inner connection, a meeting with our deeper truths. Solitude invites us to befriend ourselves, to become comfortable with our own company. This relationship with oneself is crucial because it lays the foundation for all other connections. How can we truly connect with others if we have not first connected with ourselves? How can we offer understanding, patience, or compassion to others if we have not cultivated these qualities within our own hearts during moments of solitude?

Ironically, the more we embrace solitude, the richer our connections with others become. Solitude teaches us how to be present, how to listen, and how to appreciate silence. It offers us a space to reflect on our relationships and the ways in which we engage with others. It also teaches us that connection is not just about physical proximity or constant interaction it is about the quality of presence, the ability to truly see and be seen by another. When we are comfortable in solitude, we no longer seek connection as a means of escape, but as a choice to share the fullness of who we are.

Connection, then, becomes something deeper when born from solitude. It is not about filling a void but about meeting another from a place of fullness. When we have spent time in solitude, we approach relationships with a sense of clarity. We are less likely to project our unmet needs onto others and more likely to approach them with openness and curiosity. Connection becomes an act of mutual discovery, a space where two individuals meet not to complete each other, but to complement one another's journey.

There is also an important distinction to be made between solitude and loneliness. Loneliness is the feeling of disconnection, the sense that we are cut off from others and, in some cases, from ourselves. It is a state of lacking, of longing for companionship that isn't present. Solitude, on the other hand, is a conscious choice to be alone, to retreat into oneself not out of necessity but out of a desire for introspection and peace. Solitude can be deeply fulfilling, while loneliness often feels empty. Learning to distinguish between the two is key to understanding the value of both solitude and connection.

In many ways, solitude is a form of self-care. It is the act of retreating from the external world in order to recharge, to gather one's thoughts, and to center oneself. This process is essential, especially in a world that is constantly demanding our attention, energy, and focus. Without periods of solitude, we risk becoming drained, disconnected from our own needs, and overwhelmed by the demands of others. Solitude offers us the chance to step back, to breathe, and to reconnect with our inner selves.

When we return from these periods of solitude, we are often more present in our interactions with others. Solitude has a way of sharpening our awareness and deepening our appreciation for the moments of connection we experience. It teaches us to value quality over quantity in relationships, to seek out meaningful interactions rather than superficial ones. And when we do connect with others, it is with a sense of gratitude, for we understand that connection is not something to be taken for granted but something to be cherished.

At its core, solitude and connection are about balance. Too much solitude, and we risk becoming isolated, withdrawn from the richness that comes from human interaction. Too much connection, and we risk losing ourselves in the noise of others' expectations and desires. It is in the balance of these two states that we find harmony a life that is both deeply introspective and richly connected to the world around us.

In solitude, we learn to listen. In connection, we learn to speak. Solitude allows us to process our experiences, while connection allows us to share them. Both are necessary for a full, meaningful life. Without solitude, we may never truly understand ourselves. Without connection, we may never fully experience the beauty of sharing our lives with others. The two are not in conflict; they are complementary forces that, when balanced, lead to a deeper understanding of life itself.

The modern world often pushes us toward constant connection through technology, social media, and an ever-increasing emphasis on networking. But true connection, the kind that nourishes the soul, requires solitude as its foundation. It is in those quiet moments of reflection that we come to understand who we are and what we have to offer. And when we emerge from solitude, we bring that understanding into our relationships, enriching both our own lives and the lives of those we encounter.

Ultimately, solitude and connection are both gifts. Solitude offers us the chance to meet ourselves, to nurture our inner world, and to cultivate the qualities that make us who we are. Connection allows us to share that inner world with others, to create bonds that bring meaning and joy to our lives. Neither is complete without the other. Together, they form the delicate balance that leads to a life of depth, richness, and fulfillment.

Reflections 12

Solitude,
a quiet companion,
a space where the world falls
away,
and I am left
with nothing but my own
thoughts,
the echo of my breath,
the rhythm of my heart
beating softly
in the silence.

There is a peace in being alone,
a stillness that holds
the chaos at bay,
a gentle retreat
into the self,
where the noise of the world
dissolves
and all that remains
is the simple act
of being.

In solitude,
I meet myself
without the layers,
without the masks
I wear for others.
Here, I am raw,
unfinished,
a work in progress,
a whisper of a soul
finding its way.

It is a place of reflection,
of looking inward
and seeing the shadows
and the light,
the scars of past hurts
and the soft glow of healing.
Solitude does not ask me
to be anything but real, honest,
true.
The world beyond
may be a constant storm,
but in solitude,
I am the calm
at the center,

the eye of the hurricane
where time slows,
where I can breathe
without the weight
of expectation.

Sometimes,
solitude is a gentle friend,
a welcome escape,
a chance to gather
the scattered pieces
of my heart,
to sit quietly
with the mess of it all
and just be.

Other times,
it is a mirror,
showing me the parts of myself
I'd rather not see,
the fears that linger
in the quiet corners,
the doubts that whisper
in the dark.
But even then,
there is a comfort

in knowing that I am whole,
even in my brokenness.

Solitude teaches me
that I am enough,
that within me
is a universe
of thoughts,
of dreams,
of hopes
that do not need
to be shared to be real.
It is a reminder
that I am complete,
even when alone.

In the embrace of solitude,
I find the freedom
to explore the depths
of whom I am,
to listen to the quiet voice
that so often gets lost
in the noise.
It is a sanctuary,
a refuge
where I can rest

and rebuild,
a place where the self
can breathe
without fear.

Solitude is not loneliness
it is a choice,
a gift
I give myself
to connect
with the essence
of being.

It is the art
of standing still
while the world spins on,
of finding peace
in the quiet moments
between breaths.

Here, in this space,
I am my own anchor,
my own safe harbor,
my own gentle reminder
that sometimes,
all I need
is the silence,
the solitude,
to remember who I am.

The Eternal Return

Life is filled with moments that seem random, unconnected, and fleeting. We experience joy, pain, love, and loss in ways that feel transient, as if time is nothing more than a line that moves forward without end. Yet, as I reflect more deeply on the nature of existence, I begin to wonder: what if everything we experience is not a one-time occurrence, but part of an eternal cycle that repeats, over and over, without end? This concept of the eternal return an idea that offers a profound lens through which to view life, one that challenges our usual understanding of time and existence.

The eternal return invites us to consider the possibility that every moment, every action, every decision we make is part of an endless loop. It suggests that our lives, in their entirety, will be lived again and again, exactly as they are now. This is a deeply unsettling thought for many, as it implies that the mistakes we've made, the pain we've endured, and the moments we wish we could forget will come back to us, not once, but infinitely. And yet, within this unsettling vision of time lies an extraordinary opportunity: to live in such a way that we would welcome the eternal return with open arms.

 To understand the eternal return, we must first recognize the cyclical nature of existence. Nature itself is built on cycles the cycle of the seasons, the cycle of birth and death, the cycle of the moon. Everything in the universe moves in patterns, in rhythms that repeat. Day becomes night, and night becomes day. Spring gives way to summer, then fall, then winter, and then the cycle begins again. Even our bodies are governed by cycles the rhythm of our breath, the beating of our hearts, the rise and fall of energy throughout the day. The universe seems to be telling us that life is not linear but cyclical, and that what we experience now is simply one iteration of an infinite number of iterations. But what does this mean for how we live our lives? If we truly embraced the idea that everything we do will be repeated for eternity, how would that change the way we approach each day? Would we live more intentionally, knowing that every choice we make carries the weight of infinite repetition? Or would we fall into despair, knowing that our suffering will return again and again? The eternal return forces us to confront the value of each moment and to ask ourselves whether we are living in a way that we would want to relive forever.

There is a certain heaviness to the idea of the eternal return, a sense of being trapped in a never-ending loop. But there is also a profound liberation in this concept. If every moment of our lives will recur infinitely, then every moment becomes infinitely meaningful. The smallest actions the conversations we have, the thoughts we think, the way we treat others take on a weight that is difficult to grasp. Suddenly, life is not just a series of fleeting moments, but a tapestry of eternal significance. Each thread we weave into the fabric of our existence will be part of that tapestry forever.

This realization can lead to a deep sense of responsibility. If everything we do matters for eternity, then how can we justify living in a way that is thoughtless or destructive? The eternal return demands that we confront the consequences of our actions, not just in the short term, but in the infinite long term. It forces us to ask ourselves whether we are living authentically, whether we are making choices that align with our deepest values and desires, or whether we are simply moving through life on autopilot, hoping for something better in the future.

Yet, the eternal return is not just about the weight of our choices; it is also about the acceptance of what is. If life is truly cyclical, then everything we experience both the good and the bad is part of an eternal rhythm. This means that suffering, too, is part of the cycle. We will face hardship, loss, and pain, not just once, but again and again. But within this suffering lies a hidden gift: the opportunity for growth, for transformation, for the cultivation of resilience and wisdom. The eternal return teaches us that suffering is not something to be avoided or feared but something to be embraced as an integral part of the human experience.

In this way, the eternal return mirrors the philosophy of Stoicism, which teaches us to accept what is beyond our control and to focus on how we respond to life's challenges. If we know that pain and loss will return to us endlessly, then we can stop fighting against them and instead learn to face them with grace and courage. The eternal return reminds us that life is not meant to be easy or perfect, but to be lived fully, with all of its highs and lows. It is through this full engagement with life that we find meaning and purpose.

At the same time, the eternal return invites us to cherish the moments of joy and beauty that we experience. If these moments will return to us forever, then they become sacred, something to be savored and appreciated. The laughter of a friend, the warmth of the sun on our skin, the feeling of accomplishment after a hard day's work these are the moments that make life worth living, and the eternal return encourages us to hold onto them, knowing that they will come back to us again and again. But perhaps the most important lesson of the eternal return is the call to live in the present moment. If life is a cycle, then the present moment is both the beginning and the end, the point at which everything converges. The eternal return teaches us that the past and the future are illusions, mere repetitions of what is happening now. The only reality is the present, and it is in this moment that we have the power to shape our lives. By embracing the present fully, we align ourselves with the eternal cycle of existence and find peace in the knowledge that everything we experience is part of a greater whole.

In my own life, the concept of the eternal return has forced me to reflect on the choices I make and the way I approach each day. There are moments when I feel overwhelmed by the thought of reliving my mistakes, my regrets, my pain. But there are also moments when I find deep solace in the idea that the beauty I experience the love I share, the kindness I offer, the joy I feel will come back to me in infinite waves. The eternal return has taught me that life is not something to be rushed through or taken for granted, but something to be lived with intention and gratitude.

The eternal return is not a curse but a gift. It offers us the chance to live our lives with a sense of purpose, to see each moment as an opportunity to create something meaningful. It reminds us that life is not linear, that time does not move in one direction, but that everything we experience is part of an eternal cycle. By embracing this truth, we can find peace in the knowledge that nothing is ever truly lost, that everything we do matters, and that the gift of life, in all its complexity and beauty, is something to be cherished forever.

The eternal return is, in the end, a call to live with intention, to embrace both the joys and the struggles of life, and to recognize that each moment carries within it the potential for eternity. It asks us to look at our lives through a lens of infinite recurrence and to live in such a way that we would gladly relive our existence, again and again. In doing so, we find a profound sense of meaning and connection to the cyclical nature of the universe itself, and we come to understand that life is, indeed, a gift one that we are privileged to experience, now and forever.

A Letter to the Self

In this quiet moment, I turn inward, not just to speak to myself but to you, the deepest part of me, the soul that has carried me through every moment of life. You have been with me since the beginning, silently guiding me through the twists and turns of existence. Though I often forget to acknowledge your presence, I know you are always there, waiting, listening, urging me to see more clearly and live more authentically.

I wonder how you've endured the storms I've created. The moments when I turned away from you, seeking validation outside myself, drowning in doubt, fear, or anger. In these moments, I lost sight of the truth you hold the truth that all I've ever needed was already within. And yet, you've been patient with me. You've let me stumble, make mistakes, and even break apart at times, knowing that through those cracks, I would eventually see the light you've been offering all along.
I've always felt the tension between what I think I should be and who I truly am. There's a voice in my mind, so often loud and insistent, that tells me I need to be more, more

successful, more liked, more in control. It's as if I'm constantly chasing an image of perfection that I can never quite catch. But then there's you, quietly reminding me that perfection is not the point. You whisper that I am enough, as I am, even in my brokenness, even in my vulnerability. You remind me that the journey is not about becoming more, but about remembering who I already am.

I've come to realize that the greatest challenge I face is not the obstacles outside of me, but the struggle to align my life with your quiet wisdom. You see things differently than my mind does. While I am caught up in the rush of daily life, the endless striving, you remain rooted in the present, in the now. You know that peace is not something to be earned but something to be uncovered, something that exists beneath the layers of fear, doubt, and distraction.

How many times have I ignored you? How often have I silenced your voice because it asked me to slow down, to look inward, to face truths I wasn't ready to see? I know I've betrayed you in those moments when I acted out of fear, when I let others define my worth, when I sought external approval rather than listening to the quiet strength you offer. And yet, you've never abandoned me. You've waited for me, always knowing that I would eventually return to you, because you are the core of who I am.

In those rare moments when I have listened to you really listened life has taken on a different quality. Everything becomes clearer, calmer, more real. I've felt a sense of peace that transcends the chaos of the world around me. I know that you are the source of that peace, and that it is always available, if only I remember to turn toward you. You are the wellspring of wisdom, and all I have to do is draw from it, to trust that you know the way, even when my mind doesn't.

I've learned that listening to you requires courage. It's not easy to quiet the noise of the world, to turn away from the endless distractions and demands that pull me in a thousand directions. It's not easy to sit with myself, to confront the fears, insecurities, and wounds that I've spent so long avoiding. But I know that facing these things is the only way to heal, and that healing is the path to true freedom. You've shown me that freedom is not found in escaping pain, but in embracing it, understanding it, and ultimately transcending it.

There are moments when I feel disconnected from you, when I'm overwhelmed by the world, when I question everything. In those moments, I feel lost, as if I've strayed too far from home. But even then, I know you are there, waiting for me to return. You are the constant, the eternal part of me that cannot be lost, no matter how far I may wander. And when I finally quiet the noise and turn inward, I find you there, patiently reminding me of what matters most.

I've come to see that our relationship is the most important one in my life. It's the foundation for everything else, for how I move through the world, how I relate to others, how I experience joy, love, and even sorrow. When I'm connected to you, everything else falls into place. I'm able to move through life with a sense of purpose, clarity, and peace. I'm able to love more fully, to give more freely, and to live more authentically. But when I lose touch with you, everything feels off-kilter, as if I'm living someone else's life rather than my own. So, what do I need to do to stay connected to you, my soul? I need to make space for you. I need to slow down, to quiet my mind, and to create moments of stillness where I can hear your voice. I need to trust you more, to let go of the need for control and certainty, and to embrace the mystery of life. I need to stop seeking validation outside of myself and instead find my worth in the truth that you already know that I am enough, just as I am.

I also need to forgive myself. I've been hard on myself for not living up to some imagined ideal, for making mistakes, for failing at times. But you remind me that these so-called failures are part of the journey. You remind me that growth comes not from avoiding mistakes, but from learning from them. You teach me that self-compassion is not weakness, but strength. And you show me that the path forward is not about perfection, but about presence about being fully here, fully alive, and fully myself.

As I write this letter to you, I feel a deep sense of gratitude. Gratitude for your patience, for your wisdom, for your unwavering presence in my life. I know that I will stray from you again, that I will get caught up in the noise and the rush of life. But I also know that you will always be there, waiting for me to return. And in the end, that's all I need to remember that I can always come home to you.

About the Author

Sir Ruff is an author committed to exploring the depth and complexity of human emotions and experiences. With a passion for understanding the nuances of life's most profound moments, he writes with honesty and empathy, inviting readers to journey alongside him. His newest work, *Reflecting upon Fear & Faith*, marks his second published book, following the impactful release of *The Faces of Love*. This new book further solidifies his voice as a thoughtful and reflective writer dedicated to uncovering the intricate balance between faith and doubt.

In *Reflecting upon Fear & Faith,* Sir Ruff dives into themes that resonate deeply with readers who grapple with life's uncertainties and the dualities of hope and fear. His writing is characterized by its introspective quality and its ability to provoke meaningful reflection on the nature of belief, courage, and the struggles we face within ourselves. By addressing these universal experiences, Sir Ruff creates a space where readers can find both solace and strength in their own journeys.

    His first book, *The Faces of Love,* laid the foundation for his exploration of the human heart, capturing the complexity and beauty of love in its many forms. His approach to storytelling is both poetic and raw, allowing readers to engage with his work on a deeply personal level. Building on this foundation, his latest book offers a contemplative look at the tension between faith and fear, inviting readers to explore their inner conflicts and find their own path to reconciliation.

Made in the USA
Columbia, SC
26 January 2025

1a1cb0c6-b046-4c9a-98cc-93324054725cR01